Child-Rearing and Personality Development

Child-Rearing and Personality Development

Second Edition

Paul D. Meier, M.D.,
Donald E. Ratcliff, Ed.S.,
and
Frederick L. Rowe, M.D.

Baker Books
A Division of Baker Book House Co.
Grand Rapids, Michigan 49516

Published by Baker Books
a division of Baker Book House Company
PO Box 6287, Grand Rapids, Michigan 49516-6287

Printed in the United States of America

Library of Congress Cataloging-in-Publication Data

Meier, Paul D.
Child-rearing and personality development / Paul D. Meier, Donald E. Ratcliff, and Frederick L. Rowe. — 2nd ed.
p. cm.
Rev. ed. of: Christian child-rearing and personality development. c1977.
Includes index.
ISBN 0-8010-6305-1
1. Child development 2. Child rearing I. Ratcliff, Donald. II. Rowe, Frederick L. III. Meier, Paul D. Christian child-rearing and personality development. IV. Title.
HQ769.M39 1993
649'.1—dc20 93-23808

Contents

Introduction

Bill and June couldn't help but notice how the new neighbors treated their children. "Get into the house this minute," bellowed the mother to a four-year-old who was covered with mud. "I don't wanna," the equally irate youngster responded. Meanwhile, a six-month-old screamed inside the house. "You get in here right now or I'll beat your bottom." The preschooler couldn't care less. "Oh, shut up," he said. The exchange of yells continued for several minutes, and eventually the mother brought a sandwich out to the child, who promptly threw it on the ground. "I want ice cream!" the youngster demanded. "When we have kids, I sure never want to be like that," Bill commented. June nodded her head, yet there was an inner pang of sympathy for the woman who appeared to be overwhelmed with child-rearing. They both wondered, "how can we do better?" never suspecting that the neighbor wondered the same thing.

In today's local newspaper I read horrible stories about the abuse of two children. The first was only seven weeks old, but had already suffered broken bones, mutilation, and sexual abuse. After being hospitalized several times, only to be sent home for more abuse, the child was killed by its parents. The second child was also murdered by parents, using the metal post from a bed. Tonight I watched a television program on abuse and neglect of children in day-care centers. The program suggested that these problems are far more prevalent than anyone would suspect.

These extremes shake us, and so they should. If the people in the stories really understood children, wouldn't they have acted differently? At the same time I know that many parents in our society are uncomfortable with the way they rear their children. With most of us only having one or two children, by the time we get some experience we have finished the job. We may not abuse our kids, but perhaps we wonder if we disciplined them the best way. We may not neglect them, but just maybe we feel a twinge of guilt now and then about not spending enough time with them. Parenthood can be frustrating for anyone, but especially for parents who want their faith to shape the way they treat their children, and who want their children to affirm that faith.

I read the first edition of this book shortly after it was published in 1977. I was impressed that this was, without question, the most scholarly, biblical, yet readable account of child-rearing and development I had ever read. It definitely set the pace (along with James Dobson's work) for many future books on the topic. Even as I write this, 15 years later, that original edition is still head and shoulders above the rest. The fact that it went through twenty reprintings shows that a lot of people must have agreed with me! It is a great privilege to be able to do some summarizing, rearranging, updating, and expanding of the original work. We have also tried to make it even more readable for the average parent.

This book will attempt to accomplish two huge tasks. First, we want to help Christians develop biblically sound parenting skills. Second, we want to outline some of the aspects of child development that will encourage a better understanding of children. A knowledge of what your kids can and cannot do at different ages should, in turn, help you to be a better parent. We need to know what to expect of children, but not expect more than they can reasonably produce. An accurate understanding of youngsters can also help us marvel at the beautiful, though sometimes difficult, creations God has loaned us, our children.

The first edition of this book was an outgrowth of a graduate class in personality development taught by Paul Meier. It was the first of many books he was to author and coauthor over the years. Dr. Meier, cofounder of the Minirth-Meier Clinic, blended his own training, experience as a houseparent in a youth home for delinquent and disturbed children, and other professional counseling experience with his own parenting of three children. When he wrote the first edition, all of his children were school-age or younger.

I am also the parent of three children, all school-age or younger. This is the third book I have worked on with Dr. Meier (the other two included Dr. Frank Minirth as coauthor). My work on the revision is the result of my training and teaching in child psychology, as well as my personal experience as a parent. Dr. Meier's experience in counseling and my emphasis on normal development complement one another in many areas.

In this new edition, a chapter by Dr. Fred Rowe—a child psychiatrist at one of the Minirth-Meier clinics—provides helpful information for parents who suspect that counseling might be needed for their children. When is a problem severe enough to warrant therapy? Chapter seven also suggests what the parent can expect from a good counselor.

We have been appalled by the number of psychologically disturbed Christians who were reared by relatively normal Christian parents. These parents, however, often used very poor judgment in their child-rearing. Their judgment was not only psychologically unsound, but even more important, scripturally unsound. As a result, we have written this book integrating scores of scriptural passages with hundreds of research studies on healthy and unhealthy child-rearing techniques. We have also drawn lessons from our counseling work, experiences of our students, and our own child-rearing.

We have seen many dramatic changes in the families who have put these scriptural and psychologically sound principles into practice. It is our sincere hope that soon-to-be married and young married couples, in particular, will read this book while their children are young. It is our firm belief that much of the adult personality is formed during childhood, especially the first six years. This is not to say that it is too late to correct emotional problems in adulthood. No, it is not too late, but it becomes increasingly more difficult the older one is. What takes minor correction in early childhood, takes even stronger measures in later childhood, and the same problem may require extensive counseling if not dealt with until adulthood.

This book is intended to prevent problems that often show up in psychiatric clinics and in counselor's offices. We are thoroughly convinced that if parents will get the help they need (personally and in their marriages) and use biblically sound child-rearing methods, the next generation will be far better off than we are today. It is always easier to prevent problems in the first place than to cure them after they develop.

Donald Ratcliff
Toccoa Falls, Georgia

For general information about Minirth-Meier Clinic office locations, counseling services, educational resources, and hospital programs, call (toll free) 1-800-545-1819.

The national headquarters of the Minirth-Meier Clinic is at 2100 North Collins Boulevard, Richardson, Texas 75080. Telephone numbers are (214) 669-1733 and 1-800-229-3000.

Clinics are located in Austin, Belton, Fort Worth, Houston, Sherman, Longview, San Antonio, and Waco, Texas; Albuquerque, New Mexico; Wheaton, Illinois; Little Rock, Arkansas; Springfield, Missouri; Arlington, Virginia; Seattle, Washington; Denver, Colorado, and Gardena, Laguna Hills, Newport Beach, Orange, Palm Springs, Roseville, and Santa Anna in California.

1

Preparing to Parent

All parents and parents-to-be need to improve their parenting skills. Every parent is "preparing to parent." We expect doctors to have many years of education before they begin to practice, and we also expect those in practice to update their skills regularly. Should we expect less of the most important task we can have—rearing children?

Before we go farther, let's see what kind of parent you are now (or might be in the future). Mark the response you think you would most likely make in each of these situations.

1. For the first time in her life you place a small piece of lasagna on your fifteen-month-old's tray. "Try some of this yummy

new food," you say. The youngster picks up the food, examines it curiously, then states, "no like." You then:

A. slap the child and demand she eat it.
B. ignore the statement and continue eating.
C. say, "You don't like the food? That's ok" and take it off the plate.
D. say, "You might not like the food, but you should at least try it."

2. Your preschooler has been watching his favorite TV show. It ends at bedtime, but he pleads "Will you read me a story?" You respond:

A. "Forget it, you know the rule about bedtime."
B. "I don't have time to read you a story."
C. "Whatever you want, sweetheart." After the story is read, the same request results in another story, and then another.
D. "One short story, but then it's to bed." And you follow through, regardless of protests.

3. Your school-age daughter is again complaining about doing her homework. "Why should I do this stuff?" she asks. You respond:

A. "Because that's what the teacher says, and that's just the way it is."
B. "Go ask your mother" (or father if you are the mother).
C. "Tell me how you feel about it." After all, you reason, feelings are more important than whether it gets done every day.
D. "I know it gets boring, but very few things in life are interesting all the time."

4. Your thirteen-year-old son rushes into the room. "There's gonna be a terrific party at Ron's house tonight, can I go?" You ask, "will there be girls there?" and he answers, "yeah, I think so." "Will any of the kids be drinking?" He hangs his head a bit. "I don't know for sure." You then ask, "will his parents be there?" and your son says "no, they're on vacation." You decide to:

A. ground him for even suggesting such a thing.

B. let him go—after all, you need a quiet evening alone.
C. let him make up his own mind, so he will become more responsible.
D. talk with him about the dangers of such a situation, and then calmly say "not without a responsible adult present."

Four Styles of Parenting

What kind of parent do you plan to be? What kind of parent are you already? Researchers (Schaeffer 1959, Maccoby and Martin 1983, Baumrind 1990) have found at least four styles of parenting based upon how demanding and responsive the parents are. Look at Chart 1-1 as we consider the various styles of parenting.

The first style is called the *authoritarian* approach. These rigid parents demand a lot of their children and have quite a bit of control over them. However, they are less sensitive to the needs and desires of the kids, so they are not as responsive to them. Authoritarian parents want obedience and will punish their children, often severely, if they do not immedi-

Chart 1-1. Parenting Styles

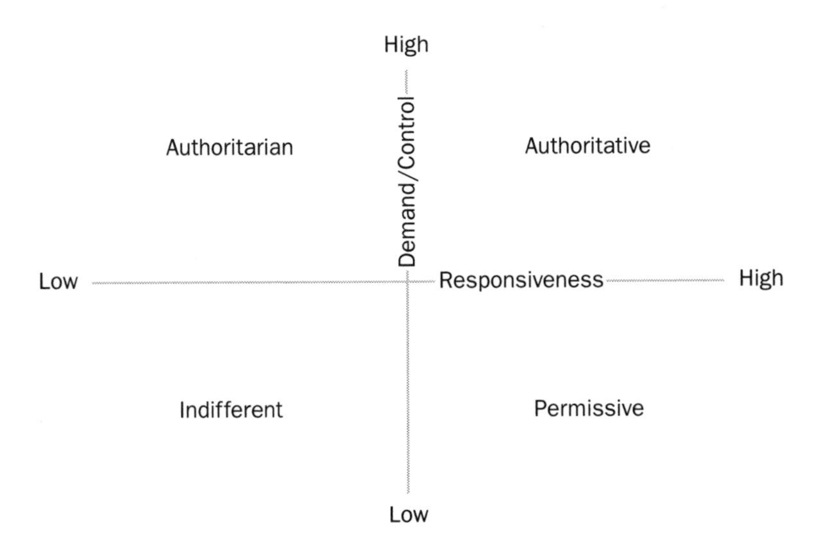

ately obey. They have little or no concern about helping their children become independent and self-sufficient. Children are expected to accept what the parent requires without question; parents rarely if ever explain why a rule is made. The authority of the parents is supreme. If the young child breaks a beautiful vase, these parents immediately spank the child without any explanation or concern about whether it was an accident or not. If you marked mostly "As" in the quiz at the beginning of this chapter, you probably are (or will be) this kind of parent.

Moving down the chart, the *indifferent* parent makes very few demands upon the child, but like the authoritarian parent does not respond much to the child's needs or wants. They are simply uninvolved with their children, preferring to spend most of their time with other things. The idea of being an involved parent is too inconvenient, and the idea of setting rules (or at least enforcing them) seems a waste of time. If anyone does much parenting, it is probably the grandparents, neighbors, or babysitters. These kids are likely to be left at an all-day infant care center from even the earliest months of life. When the flower vase gets knocked over, these parents may yell at the child but do nothing else, or else they are not there to react. You are probably inclined toward this style if you marked mostly "Bs" on the quiz.

Across the chart from the indifferent is the *permissive* parent. They are far more concerned about the needs and wants of their children, but they make few demands upon them. As with indifferent parenting, the kids are often out of control, even though the parents want to help them. They may not even expect the children to obey them; they want to be friends not parents to their children. Mom and dad try to reason with the kids and let them have a lot of input into the decisions that are made—indeed, sometimes the children make most of the decisions in this kind of family. But there are few standards and rules for these youngsters, and so they basically do what they want. The broken vase in this home brings concern for the child, even if he or she broke it on purpose. Permissive parents tend to mark "Cs" on the quiz.

Authoritative parents have strong expectations of their children, and so they make and enforce rules. They are clearly in control, but they are also realistic in their expectations. They are sensitive to the characteristics of children at different ages and want to know what the child needs and wants. The needs of the child are more important than holding to every rule in every situation, but when the child's desires and rules conflict the wants of a child are generally overruled by parental standards. Parental reasoning is combined with parental control. There is some give and take in discussions, but parents have the final say. No two children are considered to be alike, and independence is encouraged within the limits set by parents. These parents react to the broken vase by asking the children how it happened, describing their own feelings about losing it, and punishing the deed if it was intentional or encouraging the child to be more careful if it was an accident. If you marked "D" to most of the questions on the quiz, this is probably your style.

Just because two parents have the same parenting style does not mean they are exactly alike. Some authoritative parents demand and control more than others and some respond more than others. There can be many other differences as well, of course. One parent can demand a lot in the child's school life, but not in the area of athletic ability, while another parent could reverse these. But the four styles at least give us a general way of understanding some of the differences in parenting.

With each of the four styles of parenting there is also a seriously unhealthy extreme. If an authoritarian parent is extremely demanding and controlling but makes almost no response to the child's needs and desires, the danger is cruelty. That is, the parent is in the extreme upper left-hand corner of the chart. The indifferent parent makes almost no demands or has very little control over the child, while making little response to them, runs the risk of neglect. Neglect, which with cruelty is considered a form of child abuse, would be way down in the lower left-hand corner of the chart. Parents who never control their children, yet always try to give in to their desires, are likely to indulge ("spoil") them. Put them in the extreme lower right-hand corner. Highly demanding and controlling parents who are very responsive to their children run the risk of overprotecting their kids. They are in the extreme upper right-hand corner. There are seriously unhealthy extremes with all four styles of parenting.

Which Style Is Best?

As we look at the chart, what kind of parenting is most biblical? Over and over the Bible is very clear that parents must exercise control over their children (we deal with this at length in chapter 3). Yet the Bible also seems to suggest that we should be sensitive and responsive to the child's needs. For example, Ephesians 6:4 says that Christian parents must not exasperate their children. This may imply that reasoning with and listening to children are important. Proverbs 29:19 might suggest that explanations, appropriate to the age of the child, are important (though we should insist upon obedience even if the child does not understand why). Certainly the father of the prodigal son was highly responsive, both in giving him the inheritance and in the warm welcome home. God's concern for children is quite evident throughout Scripture. They are gifts from God (Ps. 127:3). The disciples thought Christ was too busy for children, and may have thought that "children should be seen and not heard." Yet Jesus rebuked the disciples for this attitude (Mark 10:14), and insisted upon holding the children (Mark 9:36; 10:13, 16), healing them (Matt. 17:18; Mark 9:27), and encouraging others to welcome them (Matt. 18:5). Children are examples of humility that should be imitated (Matt. 18:3–4). Taken as a whole, these Bible verses would suggest that parents should be responsive to their children. The authoritative style of parenting seems to be the most biblical.

A number of research studies have been conducted on these four styles of parenting. Permissive and authoritarian homes are more likely to produce children that have a wide variety of severe psychological disturbances (Rousell and Edwards 1971). Hall, Lamb, and Perlmutter (1986, 405–06) have summarized much of the research on the most common results of different parenting styles. Children reared with the authoritarian style are often overly dependent, with hostility likely by boys, and withdrawal, low self-expectations, and lack of goals by girls. Children whose parents use the indifferent style often have high amounts of aggression, obey less, and demand more. The permissive style of parenting is more likely to produce children who, like children of authoritarian parents, are hostile, withdrawn, or dependent. They are especially unlikely to tolerate frustration very well. As might be expected, the biblically preferred authoritative form of parenting has far more positive results in the research. Social responsibility and a healthy amount of independence characterize these children.

Characteristics of Mentally Healthy Families

We have seen that demand, control, and responsiveness (without overprotection) are aspects of good *parenting*. When we look at mentally healthy *families*, we find characteristics that tell much the same story, but also give us a more complete view of what good parenting is all about. A home with these five factors is more likely to help children grow into adults who will be happy and mature, both emotionally and spiritually.[1]

1. These five factors are described in the following research studies: Aston and London (1972), Bennett (1968, 1971a, 1971b), Clavan and Vatter (1972), Ford and Herrick (1974), Gerber (1973), Greenbaum (1973), and McDanald (1967). They are also considered at a more popular level by Christenson (1970), Getz (1974), Gothard (1972 and 1973), Hunt (1970), Merideth, Timmons, and Dillow (1973), and Narramore (1968).

Chart 1-2. Percentage of Children with Psychological Problems

Marriage Relationship	Parent-Child Relationship: GOOD	Parent-Child Relationship: POOR
GOOD	5%	25%
POOR	40%	90%

Love

Mentally healthy families have parents who love their children and love one another. In fact, some research suggests that the parents loving each other is even more important than their love for the youngsters. Look at Chart 1-2.

The above research by Michael Rutter (1971) shows that the lowest number of psychological problems is found in families where parents have good relationships with one another and their children, while the highest number of problems is where both relationships are weak. But if you compare the other two boxes, the children are more likely to have problems when the parents do not get along—even more problems than if the parents do not have a good relationship with the kids!

One of the main reasons that troubled parent-child relationships develop is that there is already a psychologically disturbed relationship between the husband and wife. Sometimes when a mother brings her disturbed child to Paul Meier, he puts the mother on tranquilizers and the child gets better! Most of the time children improve when parents learn better ways to live and love. If the husband and wife are not getting their love needs met by their mates, they will look elsewhere for satisfaction.

To see how a poor marriage can seriously harm children, consider the story of Ron and June (this account combines the stories of several actual couples). Ron becomes involved with another woman (or perhaps is overly involved with his work) and so June turns to her son Tommy to provide the missing love of her husband. The love she wants from Tommy is very unhealthy, however. June is so desperate for love that she becomes afraid to spank Tommy; she reasons that spanking might cause the child to stop loving her for a few minutes. She insists that Tommy sleep with her, literally taking the place of Ron. June becomes overprotective, unconsciously not wanting Tommy to grow up, because she has an unrecognized fear that he will leave her eventually, ending the only love relationship June has. Tommy is smothered with attention and is never allowed independence. Tommy becomes afraid of school because he is so overinvolved with his mother psychologically. Later, as a teenager, Tommy turns to drugs and alcohol because of the unconscious desire to escape the unhealthy relationship with his mother. Tommy hates his mother, at least unconsciously, and remains emotionally immature—perpetually childish, just as June encouraged him to be. If Tommy marries and has children, June will attempt to manipulate and smother the grandchildren and divide the parents. The unhealthy pattern affects generations to come, simply because June and Ron did not love one another in a healthy manner.

If, in contrast, it is the mother who refuses to love the father, he may react in a somewhat similar pattern, sometimes with the addition of a sexual relationship with a child or another woman. Or he may retreat from the husband-wife relationship by getting too involved with work. Another possibility is that he may leave the unhealthy relationship through desertion or divorce.

What is love, anyway? Genuine love does not develop without help; it is learned. Love requires some degree of maturity; children have an immature variety of love that is still quite selfish, and sometimes they try to use it to manipulate and avoid punishment. Within marriage, genuine love is *emo-*

tional—a feeling that is rekindled from time to time by acting in a loving manner. Sometimes there are contrary emotions in marriage, such as anger, but anger does not become sin unless the husband and wife fail to deal with it before bedtime (Eph. 4:26). Holding grudges can interfere with genuine love (Col. 3:19). Marital love is also *physical,* involving gentle caresses and consummating in sexual union (1 Cor. 7:3–5). Finally, love is *spiritual,* seen in showing patience, being kind, seeking the other person's benefit, and expecting nothing in return (1 Cor. 13). This level of mature love, with all three aspects, is found in only a minority of adults; very few people ever reach their true love potential in the marriage relationship.

While genuine love between the parents is extremely important for the mental health of children, it is also important that parents love the children. Parental love includes the spiritual aspects mentioned above. It is also physical, with plenty of hugs and kisses. Children must have attention and stimulation: if they can't get it by good behavior, they will get it by bad behavior. Parents who praise their child frequently for good behavior—such as sharing with brothers and sisters—will encourage that good behavior. Paul Meier's oldest boy was praised early in life for hugging his sister (he may have sometimes squeezed her to get even with her!), and today he is one of the "huggingest" people we know. Parental love is also emotional, although—like the love in marriage—it can exist even if the person does not feel that love at a particular moment. Children need to be treated as significant people, no matter how young or immature they may be. It is easy to ignore our children and treat them as though they are unimportant. Both authors have had to work on this aspect of love, especially when writing books or watching television.

Discipline

The Bible clearly states that genuine love also includes discipline: "He who spares the rod hates his son, but he who loves him is careful to discipline him" (Prov. 13:24). When undisciplined children grow up, they are usually immature and inadequate—they break laws, they use drugs, they have improper sexual behavior, they literally bring shame to their parents (Prov. 29:15). They generally hate their parents, often before they are teenagers.

Good discipline is not just punishment, although it certainly includes punishment. Good discipline includes spanking a child when there is rebellion against parental authority. Spanking is especially appropriate for young children because it is quick and then it is over. It needs to occur immediately after the offense, so the young child knows what the punishment is for (Eccles. 8:11). Taking away privileges for something that was done wrong is better for older children, because little kids may forget what they did wrong after a few minutes and thus not understand what the punishment is all about. There are a number of other methods of discipline as well, including some that are more positive. We will consider the subject of discipline in detail throughout the chapters that follow.

Consistency

Discipline, as well as many other aspects of the child's life, needs to be as consistent as possible. A chaotic family life that is unpredictable and constantly changing is very unhealthy for children. Likewise, some children get away with doing something bad one moment, only to receive punishment for the same thing a few minutes (or hours) later. Emotional problems are not as closely linked to the amount of discipline received as they are to how consistently the discipline is given. Husbands and wives must provide a united front. If you disagree on discipline, don't do your disagreeing in front of the children. Talk it out privately and arrive at some compromise. We must be flexible as we negotiate with the spouse (someone once said, "All women, and a few great men, change their minds"!), but always be consistent with your children. A godly person "honors those who fear the Lord, who keeps his oath even when it hurts" (Ps. 15:4). Consistency, then, even when it is unpleasant, is vitally important in child-rearing.

Example

Our children learn their behavior from us. In the end, they do what we do much more than what we say they should do. Paul Meier once heard an alcoholic parent brag about the discipline he practiced with his children. The parent said he made them go to church every Sunday morning, every Sunday night, and every Wednesday night. He made them read their Bibles every day. He made them study for at least one hour every night after school. And he would not let them watch any television, because there were too many beer commercials. Unfortunately *he* did not do any of these things regularly. He was obviously setting a very poor example for his children, and in all likelihood his children turned out the very opposite of what he wanted. He was telling them one thing and practicing another. This kind of hypocrisy ruins children. To quote Dr. O. Quentin Hyder (1971, 96), a Christian psychiatrist:

> It is not surprising that, as they get older, children from Christian homes tend to rebel and fall away from the faith of their parents. They can see the hypocrisy, the inconsistency, and the prejudice in their parents' lives. Unhappily, they then tend to equate these with the church, and in rejecting their parents' faith they also reject Christ in their own lives. By contrast those Christian homes in which love is paramount produce sons and daughters who themselves devoutly propagate the faith to their own children.

The Apostle Paul told his converts to follow his example; to do as he did (Phil. 3:17). Parents who follow God's commandments not only profit personally, but also have children who profit from parental obedience because of their godly example (Deut. 5:29). Do you want your children to be truthful? Then speak the truth in love (Eph. 4:15). Do you want children to forgive one another and you for your mistakes? Then forgive them and others in your life (Eph. 4:32). Whatever qualities you want in your children need to be portrayed in your own life.

Fathering

A domineering, smothering mother and weak father lie at the root of many mental illnesses (Meier, Minirth, and Ratcliff 1992). Almost as bad is the fatherless home, either because of divorce, separation, an unwed mother, or excessive hours at work (Whitehead 1993).

God is very clear about who should lead the home. Consider these verses: “Wives, submit to your husbands, as is fitting in the Lord” (Col. 3:18), and, “For the husband is the head of the wife as Christ is the head of the church, his body, of which he is the Savior. Now as the church submits to Christ, so also wives should submit to their husbands in everything” (Eph. 5:23–24). The wife was created to be a helper for the husband (Gen. 2:18), and “he will rule over you” (Gen. 3:16). Submission, respect for the husband, purity, modesty, and a gentle quiet spirit are marks of the godly wife (1 Pet. 3:1–4).

Of course there are parallel commands for the husband: the need for consideration, respect (1 Pet. 3:7), love, and giving of self (Eph. 5:25–33). Some have suggested that this requires equality between husband and wife. The Bible *does* say men and women are equal in value: “You are all sons of God through faith in Christ Jesus . . . There is neither Jew nor Greek, slave nor free, male nor female, for you are all one in Christ Jesus” (Gal. 3:26–28). “Husbands, in the same way be considerate as you live with your wives, and treat them with respect . . . as *heirs with you* of the gracious gift of life” (1 Pet. 3:7). We are equal in importance in the eyes of the God who created us for each other. God has merely given us different responsibilities. We are made in such a way that our families will be healthiest if the husband assumes the ultimate leadership in the home. Husbands need to be able to give in once in awhile, but if you are unable to reach a compromise, God has established the husband as the leader in the home. But time and again we have seen that great hesitancy by the wife about a major change in family life can be God's attempt at redirecting the husband. Husbands need to listen carefully to the wife's opinion, and honor her views. Of course, if the husband physically abuses his wife or children, he has forfeited the right to being head of the house. The husband needs counseling, and the wife and children may need legal protection.

As we will see in subsequent chapters of this book, high quality fathering is one of the greatest needs today. Good fathers are vital to emotional and spiritual growth in children. Some of the best guidelines for fathers can be found in Scripture: "We dealt with each of you as a father deals with his own children, encouraging, comforting, and urging you to live lives worthy of God" (1 Thess. 2:11–12). The best fathers comfort their children and encourage them regularly. Spiritual development is also a strong concern of good fathers (Deut. 11:18–19).

Other Qualities of Healthy Families

Researcher Nick Stinett (1985), now at the University of Alabama, pioneered important research on what makes families strong. He believes that many of society's problems can be traced to unhealthy families. So he decided to do a thorough study of what makes families strong and happy. He looked at families throughout the United States, as well as several other countries. He also considered single-parent families, black families, and other ethnic families. Using questionnaires and interviews with 3000 healthy, strong families, six qualities consistently surfaced. In order, those characteristics are:

1. *Commitment.* The family was top priority, family members could be counted on, and each member was 100 percent for the others.
2. *Time.* What they did as a family was not always expensive or complicated, but they spent considerable time together and they enjoyed being together.
3. *Communication.* The family talked to one another quite a bit, although the conversations were not always deep or profound, and they were good listeners, even though they might sometimes have conflicts.
4. *Appreciation.* They often complemented one another; they looked for things to complement in one another.
5. *Spirituality.* Strong families saw themselves as committed spiritually, related their faith to everyday life, and most of the healthy families attended church.
6. *Problem-solving.* They could deal with crisis situations in a positive manner, sometimes with the help of others outside the family.

By combining the control/demand and responsiveness aspects of an authoritative family, with the five factors found in mentally healthy families, and the six qualities of strong families, we have some definite guidelines for becoming the best parents we can. None of us can accomplish everything at once, and we suspect that most families fall short in at least one of these areas, but perhaps the aspects that need to be worked on will be made clear by looking at the total picture.

How to Develop Emotionally Disturbed Children

Of course you don't want your children to have psychological problems. But one way to see what we should avoid in parenting is to observe some of the things parents do that can produce psychological disturbances in their children. Negative family characteristics are at the root of many psychological problems.[2] Most of these influences apply to adolescents as well as children.

Keep in mind these are trends that have been found, with many exceptions. If you were reared in some of these ways, you may have been fortunate and did not develop problems (although you might still benefit from talking with a counselor). However, since these are often linked with emotional disturbances, they are definitely to be avoided in child-rearing.

How to Develop an Alcoholic or Drug Addict

[These are also linked with other psychological problems as well]

1. Give the child everything he or she wants.
2. When the child does wrong, nag but never spank (or only spank when he or she shows signs of independence).
3. Do not allow your husband, wife, or the child's teachers to punish the child.
4. Encourage the child to be overly dependent on the parent, so drugs or alcohol will replace you when he or she gets older.
5. Make all the decisions for the child; solve all the child's problems so he or she will always run to you when the going gets tough.

2. These influences have been culled from a wide variety of studies. See Brenner (1967), Chefetz, Blane, and Hill (1971), Hoffman (1970), McNichol (1970), Nichtern (1973), Schuckit (1972), and Valliant (1971) on drug and alcohol addiction. See Gundlock (1972), Siegelman (1973), and Carson, Butcher, and Coleman (1988) on homosexuality. See Cleckley (1941), Millon and Everly (1985), Carson, Butcher, and Coleman (1988), Guze, Woodruff, and Clayton (1972), Hawkins (1975), Hoffman (1970), and Minirth (1975) on sociopathic and histrionic personalities. See Block (1969), Fish (1966), Lidz (1972), Stabenau (1968), Carson, Butcher, and Coleman (1988) on schizophrenia. See Adams (1972), Hays (1972), Salzman (1973), and Husband and Hinton (1972) on obsessive and accident-prone children. See Bruch (1971), Crisp (1970a and 1970b), and Wold (1973) on obesity and anorexia.

6. Always bail the child out of trouble; never let him or her suffer the consequences of the misbehavior.
7. Criticize the child's father or mother openly.
8. Dominate your husband or wife; it helps if at least one of you is an alcoholic.
9. Take a lot of prescription drugs, so taking illegal drugs will be easier for your child.

How to Develop a Homosexual

[The above steps 1 through 9 are often found in the family backgrounds of homosexuals as well]

10. Protect your son very carefully; never let him play football or baseball with other boys, because he might get hurt, and don't let him ever be a newspaper boy or patrol boy because he might catch pneumonia.
11. Don't let boys spend much time with their fathers or other adult males. For girls, don't let them spend time with their mothers. (In addition, youngsters are more likely to become homosexuals when their first sexual experiences are with those of the same sex, either as children or in adolescence).
12. Teach your son to sew, cook, and knit, and be sure he dislikes traditional male roles. Encourage your daughter to play football and other rough and tumble activities.
13. Be sure your son plays consistently with the neighborhood girls, or sisters and their friends. Never let your daughter play with other girls, but only with brothers and other boys.
14. Give your son a feminine name and tell him what a cute girl he would have been; you might even dress him up in his big sister's clothes when he is little. Give your daughter a masculine nickname and never encourage her to wear a dress.

How to Develop a Sociopath
(a criminal with no conscience)
[Again, follow the steps for developing an alcoholic, with the following additions or substitutions]

15. Never spank your child. That's a thing of the past, and is one of the few things considered immoral today.
16. Let your children express themselves any way they want, including temper tantrums and calling you names.
17. Let your child run your life. Allow the child to manipulate you and play on your guilt. Give in to temper tantrums, and never cross the child when he or she is angry.
18. Never enforce the household rules. That way the child will be able to choose which laws of society to break when older, and will not fear any consequences because he or she never suffered any.
19. Never require chores; do all the chores for the child. That way he or she will be irresponsible when older and blame others when things do not go well.
20. Believe or encourage lying. Tell a few lies yourself, and be sure to cheat on your income taxes.
21. Criticize others whenever possible, and never let the child associate with religious people.
22. Give the child a big allowance but don't ever make the child do anything for it. If he or she has to work for money, the child may get the idea one has to work for a living. If the child happens to do something worthwhile, always reward it with a lot of money because you would never want him or her to get the idea that responsibility is its own reward.

How to Develop a Histrionic
(someone emotionally unstable, immature, and self-centered, a problem more common among females)

[The nine steps for developing an alcoholic are also associated with this problem, but add the following]

23. Spoil your daughter and let her get her own way, especially if she pouts or cries.
24. Marry an immature husband and do not meet his sexual needs; that way he will seek warmth and affection by becoming too close to the daughter.
25. Lie to yourself a lot, so your daughter will learn that habit as well.
26. Always praise your daughter for her appearance, never for her character.
27. When your child runs away, be sure to run after her and apologize for not letting her have her way in the first place.
28. If your child pretends to be sad or fakes a suicide attempt, be sure to show her how guilty you feel for not letting her have her own way.
29. Encourage your daughter to become a movie star, because she is already a very dramatic actress.
30. Get divorced and remarried a number of times so your daughter will learn that all men are good-for-nothing. You might also live with someone you are not married to.
31. Encourage your daughter to wear the most seductive clothing you can find. She will naturally do this to please her father, who always praises her appearance rather than character, and with whom she may well be sexually involved (note: about one-third of the histrionic females treated by Paul Meier have been sexually abused by their fathers or stepfathers).
32. When your daughter comes home late from a date, scold her for her behavior, then ask her for all the exciting details and enjoy every moment of the telling, but try to hide your obvious enjoyment.

33. Reward your son or daughter whenever the child plays sick; this will help make the child a hypochondriac, which often goes with the histrionic disorder.

How to Develop a Schizophrenic
(a person seriously out of touch with reality)

[The nine steps for developing an alcoholic, again, are a start, with the following exceptions]

34. Tell the child you love him or her, but never hug or show any genuine warmth. Never let the child snuggle, even when a baby. Always be cold and impersonal when you tell the child of your love.
35. Promise the child you will do things with him or her, but always think of excuses not to when the time comes.
36. Follow the policy that husbands should be seen but not heard, and they should be seen only when they have their wives' permission.

How to Develop a Compulsive Child
(an overly rigid perfectionist)

37. Talk all the time, but don't be physically active. Never listen to what your child has to say.
38. Expect perfect manners from your child; never tolerate mistakes.
39. Don't go around other people very much, and be as critical as possible of everyone around you.
40. Be a real snob.
41. The wife should always dominate the husband.
42. Teach your child that morality should always be a way of being considered superior to others or of getting to heaven.
43. Never make any serious commitments to God and be critical of other people's religious convictions, especially the child's grandparents.

44. Tell your child the father is the boss, but always be sure the mother is really the boss.
45. Expect the child to be completely toilet trained by twelve months of age.
46. Be very careful with every penny you spend. Save for the future, and don't let the future ever come.
47. Emphasize the letter of the law, not the spirit of the law. Make your rules quite rigid and never allow any exceptions.
48. Shame your child for any interest in sexuality.

How to Develop an Accident-Prone Child

49. Get into lots of serious arguments with your spouse, especially about the child. That way the child will blame himself or herself and react to the feelings of guilt by hurting self in some way.
50. Ignore your child, especially when confidence or good character traits surface. Only notice the child when he or she gets hurt, then overreact with extreme sympathy for every scrape or bruise (because of your guilt for ignoring him or her the rest of the time).
51. Both husband and wife should be gone most of the time. Leave the child in the care of brothers and sisters, or a babysitter who does not care much for children. Always be too tired and busy to notice the child when you are at home.

How to Develop an Obese or Anorexic (Extremely Underweight) Child

52. Support every aspect of women's liberation, but often express your frustration at how little is improving for women.
53. Give your children lots of food instead of lots of love.
54. The father should be passive in the home, even if intelligent and financially successful.

55. The mother should be overweight, overprotective, and the boss in the home.
56. The wife should never show respect for the husband.
57. The mother should be dominant and restrictive. There might even be a nearby grandmother who also dominates the household.
58. Marry a husband who was bossed around by his mother and doesn't like women very much (not even sexually). It also helps if he is obsessed with his work and other activities.
59. Encourage the husband to direct his hostility toward the daughter.

There you have it: 59 ways to ruin a child. Many of these "guidelines" can also contribute to other kinds of emotional problems as well. For a thorough discussion of psychological problems, including possible causes, see Meier, Minirth, and Ratcliff (1992). We hope you will *avoid* every one of the 59!

Developing a Healthy Self-Concept

We have all been told in many ways, throughout our lives, that we are inferior. Sometimes we have been told in words, such as a child saying "You're a real dummy" to a playmate on the playground. Sometimes we are told without words, such as the ignored daughter asking her father for help while he is reading the newspaper. Some of the messages, like the child on the playground, are intentional. At other times the messages are unintentional, as represented by the father and daughter example. We believe very firmly that our first and most important calling from God, if we are parents, is to be the kind of parents that God would have us be. No matter if you are a doctor, pastor, missionary, business person, or whatever you are—your family comes first! Whatever time you have left over from being the right kind of parent, that's the time you can use to accomplish whatever other callings God has given you. And one of the most important things we can do for our children is to develop within them an emotionally healthy and scripturally accurate self-concept. Without self-worth, our children will not only have a miserable life, but they will also be unable to reach the potential given by God. Parents also need an accurate self-concept, since children tend to imitate. Misery from a poor self-concept may make it easier to act in a way that will hurt children emotionally. We saw 59 examples of this in the previous section of this chapter. We believe that all emotional pain ultimately comes from three root sources: (1) lack of self-worth, (2) lack of intimacy with others, and (3) lack of intimacy with God. A poor self-concept can significantly hamper us in all three of these essential areas.

When we speak of a healthy self-concept, there are two extremes to avoid. Many people have a poor self-concept, feeling inferior and worthless. They feel unable to do anything of value because they do not feel God gave them much to start with. They undervalue themselves, and believe God shortchanged them. Others have an exaggerated self-concept, seeing themselves as better than they really are. Psychologists sometimes call these people *narcissists.* This word comes from an ancient Greek story in which a man named Narcissus walked by a pool of water and fell in love with his own reflection. We can love ourselves in a healthy way (when it is balanced by an equal love for others—Matt. 19:19), but when we come to think we are better or more valuable than others, we fall into the sin of pride. An accurate self-concept develops by avoiding both extremes, the sin of pride and the error of a poor self-concept. We must value ourselves because God created us, but realize we are nothing apart from God.

During the first years of life, children often feel inferior because they *are* inferior in many ways. They are smaller physically, more clumsy, more ignorant of the facts, and make mistakes in their interpretation of the facts they know. They are also inferior in authority, with parents ruling over them and often older brothers and sisters bossing them around. Once they enter school, they start receiving red marks on their papers, usually marks showing them where they are wrong. Even when the teacher marks an 80 or 90 percent on the papers, they realize that means they got 20 or 10 percent wrong. Instead of emphasizing what they have learned, the overwhelming message communicated by many schools is negative—"see what you did wrong" (Glasser 1969).

False Values

Feelings of poor self-worth often come from the false values held by parents, schools, and society in general. We may tell children these values are not important, but they see the values we actually live by. What are some of these false values?

Materialism is emphasized constantly on television commercials. Most of the people portrayed on television live in very fine homes, and almost every commercial tells us we need another expensive product to make us happy. Of course the commercials are lies, most of us realize that at some level, but we still buy more and more things. The children see our spending, and they hear the bragging of their friends at school, and quickly pick up this false value. They also see our frustrations about not having more money and things, and before long they are measuring their own self-worth in their possessions: bikes, clothes, video games, and spending money. If they do not have these things, they feel worthless. Even if they have them, they can find someone with more money, a newer fancier bike, more expensive clothes, and so on, so they still feel inferior. There is no winning with materialism—unless you reject the value altogether.

We want to make it clear that it is not a sin to be rich. But it *is* a sin to base our self-worth on our riches. Some of the godliest people in the Bible were wealthy: Abraham, Joseph, David, and many others. But their self-worth was based on their faith in God, wisdom, and godly character traits. The

Apostle Paul experienced both riches and poverty, but he "learned the secret of being content . . . whether living in plenty or in want" (Phil. 4:12). The secret was rejecting the false value of materialism.

A second false value is a wrong emphasis upon *education*. There is nothing wrong with good grades, and we should encourage our children to do well in school and get all the education they can. Paul Meier learned to draw house plans when he was young, and his father rewarded him by building the house he designed and moving their family into it! That certainly contributed to his own self-worth. But we have also seen an emphasis upon education get out of hand. One man earned a Ph.D. degree from Duke university, but felt like a failure because he did not go for the M.D. degree his parents wanted. Many people with doctorates carry around bad feelings about some course where they received less than an "A." Another young man was determined to become a doctor, even when he flunked introductory biology, because his parents expected it; he was setting himself up for life-long failure and a poor self-concept. As with material wealth, there is nothing wrong with intelligence and education, as long as more important things take priority.

Some parents go to the other extreme, caring little about the accomplishments of their children. There is a place for praising our children when their grades improve. We should encourage them to get an education that honors the Lord's calling on their lives. But the person who has many years of college is not worth more to God. In fact, if a person is drawn away from spiritual things by attending a college, it might be better not to get that education (or perhaps find a better school). God can use a good education if the person is not ruined spiritually in the process, or ruined emotionally by attempting something they simply cannot accomplish.

Athletics taken to an unhealthy extreme can be another false value that sets our children up for a poor self-concept. As with education, athletic ability can be a wonderful asset and actually increase self-worth if the child does not make athletics the most important thing in life. Participating in sports can help a child by gaining the respect of peers, encouraging teamwork, helping the child learn to win graciously and accept defeat, and learning to play by the rules. A youngster can also learn that practice brings improvement. All of these positive traits can carry over to the rest of life.

But athletics can also destroy a child's self-worth. Parents and coaches who continually criticize the child's mistakes, and give little praise for doing things right are not providing the acceptance the child needs. Are parents and coaches developing character and healthy competition, or teaching a "win at any cost" philosophy that will later be applied to other areas of life? We can also ask too much of our children in this area, expecting them to succeed in areas where we were weak. Our youngsters should be encouraged to try out for sports, but if they do not make the team they should be praised for having the courage to give it a try. Neither Paul Meier nor I have a lot of natural athletic ability—much of that ability is inherited—so we both learned to do well in other areas instead. We need to teach our children the same thing: learn to compensate by doing well in the areas where you have ability.

By the way, sports are not just for boys—girls can benefit from athletics just as much as boys, but don't try to make your daughter into a boy since this can hurt her sexual identity. Some fathers prefer sons so much that their daughters try to become boys to gain their acceptance. This produces long-term emotional conflicts and can even result in sexual problems later when the daughter gets married. But do not be overly concerned if your daughter is a bit of a tomboy in the preteen years, which is fairly common. Just don't encourage her to try out for left tackle on the high school football team!

A fourth false value is an overemphasis upon *physical appearance*. This, along with materialism, is perhaps the most often promoted value in society. Again, how many commercials and television programs feature beautiful people? How many top stars (other than comedians—people we laugh at) are homely? There is nothing wrong with being beautiful, and it is noted positively several times in the Bible, but taken to the extreme an emphasis on beauty can ruin the self-concept. For example, we fear the message communicated by beauty contests, especially those for children. It won't hurt to praise your children *occasionally* for how nice they look. But, as we saw earlier in this chapter, praising appearance over and over again with no concern for character and behavior can produce life-long personality problems—the daughter (or less often, the son) may become a histrionic. When thinness is overvalued, the child may become anorexic.

Children easily learn to base self-worth on appearance. Even if the child is attractive, there is always another girl who has a prettier face, a better figure, less knobby knees, and so on. There is always a fellow who is more handsome, flexes larger muscles, and has a better voice. In many cases the more attractive the person is, the more inferior he or she feels deep down, perhaps because parents and others place more emphasis upon the child's appearance. *What a difference it would make if parents would primarily praise the child's good character and behavior!* Character and behavior are correctable, physical defects usually are not. Valuing desirable behavior and attitudes can help the child develop self-worth, which is vital to mental health.

Some children and adults do not recognize hidden bitterness and resentment toward God because God did not design us the way we would like. We need to realize God made us the way we are because he knows our appearance—whatever it is like—is basic to his purpose for our lives. We are not wiser than God; he does not make mistakes. On the other hand, we should do the best we can (without going to extremes) with what we have been given. We can usually change things like being overweight. Teenage girls can use a bit of makeup if need be. Clothes can be tasteful, clean, and ironed, even if inexpensive. We can encourage our children to correct the correctable areas of appearance, and accept the rest as part of God's plan. We can also teach them healthy compensation, learning to concentrate upon the areas where they are more gifted.

The Healthy Church

These and other false values in society contribute to a poor self-concept in children and adults. Unfortunately, certain church activities can also make children feel inferior. Even good people can fall into unhealthy religious practices.

Some active church laypeople, preachers, and missionaries are so busy helping others that their children develop terrible feelings of worthlessness. Paul Meier's sister went through a temporary stage of rebellion because her father was spending too much time doing church work and too little time with the family. Because his daughter was unruly Paul's father resigned his position (in keeping with Titus 1:6), and as a result his sister is now a godly woman who has the highest regard for the father she once rebelled against. Some have suggested that a layperson should only hold one position in the church so that job will be done well and the rest of one's spare time can be spent with the family. We think this is a great idea. Likewise, a minister or missionary who cannot say "no" sometimes for the sake of the family should serve the Lord in some other profession (1 Tim. 3:4–5; 5:8). Church members can assist their pastors by little things such as not calling them at night, hiring people to relieve them of mundane chores, and telling others about Christ and encouraging our fellow Christians rather than expecting the pastors to do it all. When all of God's people share the work of the ministry, we are following the example of the early church.

The local church you attend can become one of the major influences on your children's self-concept. If you attend a negative, legalistic church that neglects God's love and forgiveness, you need to go somewhere else! It will permanently damage your child's self-worth. These unhealthy churches somehow convey the idea that God is a mean old man holding a whip, just waiting for us to break one of his rules so he can snap us with the whip or throw us out. How very different from the loving, forgiving God in the Bible! For example, one man I know was told by his church that he would go to hell if he missed church three times in a row. After he skipped church a few weeks in childhood, he decided there was no use in returning—regardless of what he did he was convinced he was bound for hell. He did not attend church again for nearly thirty years. Fortunately, he eventually found a loving, accepting church that corrected the misconception.

On the other hand, you may be in a liberal church, hoping to save the sinking ship. You may find that your children will sink with it! Harsh churches tend to attract people who had parents who were rigid, overly demanding, critical, and punished too much. Liberal churches tend to attract people whose parents pampered and indulged them, hardly ever corrected them, and rarely punished their children. You need to be in a church where the Bible is central, where people are coming to Christ, where Christians are growing spiritually, where genuine love is practiced, where the pastor preaches both forgiveness and justice, and where healthy entertainment and other activities are available for your children and teenagers. Children are ruined by rigid churches that stand for the wrong things, or liberal churches that don't stand for anything (for other characteristics of healthy churches, see Getz 1975).

The Bible can help us find a healthy balance in church life. For example, it says that every one of us is less than perfect. We have "dross," the impurities of sin, emotional problems, and other areas of imperfection. God says, "I will thoroughly purge away your dross and remove all your impurities" (Isa. 1:25). We fall short and need improvement. But it is important to see the whole picture biblically. In Proverbs 25:4

Solomon asks God to "remove the dross from the silver, and out comes material for the silversmith." While there is dross, the basic material is silver. How beautiful that God moved Solomon to describe us as such a precious substance! Removing the dross, the sin, and other problems, results in "material for the silversmith"—pure silver for our Maker. The rigid church only sees the dross, while the liberal church only looks at the silver. We have both. Those of us who come from more rigid church backgrounds must never forget that underneath the dross, each of us (and our children) is a silver vessel. Not one of us is inferior to anyone else, although we each have a different, unique design. Every one of us is extremely important to God (Matt. 10:29–31).

A Healthy Self-Love and a Positive View of God

Sometimes parents and churches teach children that self-hatred is a virtue rather than a sin. Many people seem to believe that salvation is the result of obeying certain rules and regulations, tithing, hiding emotions, attending all church services, and constantly reminding themselves of how worthless they really are. These Christians are likely to be chronically depressed; we see them often in our counseling. They may become withdrawn from others or even become psychotic—completely out of touch with reality—because reality as they see it is too painful to bear. They may constantly worry about losing their salvation instead of having the assurance of eternal life (1 John 5:11–13). They believe God requires them to be absolutely perfect to be acceptable, so they never really feel forgiven. Those who cannot accept themselves are usually very critical of others as well—*you cannot truly love others until you learn to love yourself in a healthy way.*

What does it mean to have healthy self-love? First, the Bible recommends taking care of your body (1 Cor. 3:16; 6:19–20; 2 Cor. 6:16). Healthy eating habits, as well as adequate exercise and recreation, are crucial. We also need healthy sleeping habits—sleeping not only provides needed rest, but also allows us to dream, which can help us reduce emotional tensions (Bonine 1962, 229–30). The average adult needs between six and ten hours of sleep each night, teens need about nine or ten, elementary aged children need about ten or eleven, preschoolers about twelve, and babies about sixteen to eighteen hours each day. Recreation, such as hiking, camping, and playing games with friends is also important to self-love. Even Christ himself spent much of his three-year ministry camping out in the mountains, sometimes with his disciples and sometimes alone.

Besides promoting healthy self-love, we as parents can encourage an accurate self-concept by helping our children have an accurate view of God. The view of God is to some extent related to the concept of the parent. We need to accept our children, complete with their imperfections, spend time with them, and punish them when they do things we know are bad for them in the long run. As a result this should produce a concept of a God who is loving, accepting, listening, and disciplining. An accurate concept of God also helps our children have an accurate self-concept, because they are more likely to see themselves as they really are—which by definition is how God sees us.

True versus False Guilt

One of the things that can help children have an accurate view of God is to help them separate true and false guilt. *True guilt* is the uncomfortable, inner awareness that we have violated a moral law of God. It is partly the result of conviction by the Holy Spirit, and partly the conscience. The conscience is molded by many influences in the environment, such as what our parents taught was right or wrong, what they practiced, and what our church taught and practiced. It is also shaped by what our friends said and did, and what we learned from our teachers. The Bible can influence the conscience, although we are also influenced by our own interpretations and sometimes misunderstandings of the Bible. The Holy

Spirit is always right, but our consciences can be very wrong. If the conscience is immature, we can do something wrong and not be bothered by it because we do not know it is wrong. Or we can have an overgrown conscience and then the conscience will bother us even when God does not consider what we did to be wrong. This is called *false guilt;* feeling guilty for something that God and his Word do not condemn.

True guilt is valuable, because it leads us to repentance and right living so we can stay in fellowship with God, as well as have a better self-concept. Some people have a poor self-concept because they need to turn from their sin; they feel guilty because they *are* guilty. But others experience false guilt, especially Christians from legalistic churches. They feel guilty for things the Bible does not condemn. For example, they may feel guilty for being tempted. It's no sin to be tempted. Even Christ was tempted (Heb. 4:15). But it *is* a sin to dwell on temptation and yield to it. Paul Tournier (1962, 64) states that false guilt ". . . comes as a result of the judgments and suggestions of men. 'True guilt' is that which results from divine judgment . . . Therefore real guilt is something quite different from that which constantly weights us down, because of our fear of social judgment and the disapproval of men." Hyder (1971, 64–70) adds that "The causes of false guilt stem back to childhood upbringing . . . too rigid expectations or standards imposed by parents."

Satan's Lie

One of Satan's lies is that we are inferior and worthless. The Bible clearly states that we are "fearfully and wonderfully made" (Ps. 139:14), and that even the hairs on our head are numbered (Matt. 10:29–33). God sees us as being of value—not worthy of salvation, but worthwhile, valuable because he created us. We have no right to condemn ourselves, only God has that right, and Christians should leave judging and condemning to God alone. We need to set new goals for ourselves and our children that are realistically attainable, and no longer compare ourselves or our children with others who are more gifted in specific areas. We should compare our performance with what we believe God expects of us. God does not expect us or our children to achieve absolute perfection in this life. But he does want us to seek and follow his will for our lives to the best of our abilities (Hyder 1971, 121–22).

Parenting for Future Generations

A basic idea throughout this book is that how you rear your children makes a great deal of difference. Not only will your child-rearing affect your children, but also generations to come. Consider this warning from God: "For I, the Lord your God, am a jealous God, punishing the children for the sin of the fathers to the third and fourth generation of those who hate me, but showing love to a thousand generations of those who love me and keep my commandments" (Exod. 20:5–6).

Clearly this does not mean that the children are held responsible for what the parents do (Deut. 24:16; Ezek. 18:20). As you study healthy and unhealthy parent-child relationships, the meaning is very clear. It simply means that if we, as parents, live sinful and psychologically unhealthy lives, there will be a profound effect upon our children, grandchildren, and perhaps other descendants as well. God is not punishing our offspring for our sins, *we are,* by not living the right way. We saw this earlier in "How to Develop Emotionally Disturbed Children," and we see this in the area of the self-concept as well.

On the other hand, we need to focus our attention on the positive promise in Exodus 20:6—God promises to show "love to a thousand generations of those who love me and keep my commandments." A valuable legacy can be left for generations to come by good parenting, an inheritance more valuable than any amount of money we could leave our children.

In the chapters that follow we will continue to examine parenting, with emphasis upon age-specific aspects of child-rearing and child development. We will begin with the child before birth and progress, stage by stage, all the way to adolescence. Seeing specific characteristics and guidelines for each age group will help us in "preparing to parent."

2

A New Life Begins

Don and Brenda had been trying for a third child for several years. "Perhaps we should be satisfied with two healthy boys," they thought, but deep within both of them was a longing for a little girl to complete their family. An infertility specialist was not very encouraging. One evening they even went forward in church to have the elders pray for them—although they were too embarrassed to tell them the request for a baby.

Two weeks later a missed period produced excitement. Not too much, though, because there had been several of these false alarms before. Early one morning, Brenda assembled the pregnancy test, and waited for the answer. The minutes seemed like hours, but finally the time was up. The test was positive!

For a few moments she savored the fact that she was the only person in the whole world who knew she was pregnant. Finally she decided to wake up Don with the news. They hugged one another, and dared to ask, "But will it be a girl?"

Life Before Birth

For you created my inmost being;
you knit me together in my mother's womb.
I praise you because I am fearfully and wonderfully made;
your works are wonderful,
I know that full well.
My frame was not hidden from you
when I was made in the secret place.

Psalm 139:13–15

Long ago the psalmist reflected upon the developing child in the womb, emphasizing God's part in the process of growth. This is a particularly interesting Scripture considering the fact that little was known about how children developed before birth until the last couple of decades. In the past some even thought the baby was already formed in the father's sperm and simply grew larger as time went by. However, the recent development of photography within the womb shows how beautiful and amazing is God's "knitting."

From the uniting of egg and sperm comes new life, a cell often termed the "ovum" for the first two weeks. The original one cell multiplies repeatedly, although the total amount of space the cells take is no more than the original single cell. By the end of the first two weeks the baby is about the size of the period that ends this sentence.

At about two weeks the cells begin to look different from one another. This is because they will take on different functions with some becoming legs, others becoming the head, still others the arms, and so on. At this point the baby is called an "embryo."

Different parts of the body begin forming at different stages of development. The nervous system, including the brain and spinal cord, and the heart begin developing first. By the fourth week the arms, eyes, legs, and ears can also be seen. At six weeks portions of the mouth and the genitals are forming (Schickedanz, Hansen, and Forsyth 1990, 80).

The mother's care for the baby is extremely important at this time. She can care for her child by taking care of herself, avoiding things that can harm the child, and getting good prenatal care. Physicians have discovered that a mother's illness, injury, or exposure to chemicals, drugs, or x-rays can directly affect the unborn child. The potentially serious harm to the developing embryo is generally in the areas of the body that are developing at the time.

For example, an injury during the third week of pregnancy is most likely to affect the brain, spinal cord, or heart, and less likely to affect other areas of the body. In contrast, an injury in the eighth week is more likely to damage areas of the mouth, genitals, or ears (although defects in other areas can also result). Injury that occurs after sixteen weeks of age is likely to produce physical defects but not major structural problems.

Fathers, too, must be careful for the sake of the child. If they smoke, they need to quit as soon as possible, since children with fathers that smoke are much more likely to develop cancer (John, Savitz, and Sandler 1991). Firemen, welders, those who work with paints and solvents, and fathers in the aircraft industry may sometimes breath toxic fumes. The result can be defective sperm and children more likely to have birth defects (Davis 1991; Peters, Preston-Martin, and Yu 1981). A father's use of alcohol may possibly produce birth defects as well (Zigler and Stevenson 1993, 132).

At the ninth week the child is termed a "fetus." Now the appearance of the baby is clearly different from the fetuses of all other creatures on earth. By the twelfth week the heart is pumping blood throughout the tiny three inch, one ounce body. Four weeks later the mother can begin to feel the movements made by the fetus, although movement actually began long before this point. By twenty weeks hair begins to form (although it is often lost again prior to birth). At twenty-six weeks, six months after conception, the child is sucking, opening its eyes, and can survive outside the womb.

The last five months had been exciting but also a bit unpleasant at times for Brenda. The nausea of morning sickness had begun almost right away, but before long had subsided. Now she felt new energy because of the higher level of hormones in her blood.

At the next appointment with the doctor, the whole family watched as an ultrasound picture of the baby was made. How amazing that sound waves can be projected into a woman's body and the reflections make up a picture. "What will it be, a girl or a boy?" Brenda asked. "I cannot be absolutely certain, of course, but it sure looks female to me." Five-year-old Stephen asked, "Does that mean it's a girl or a boy?"

From this point until birth the child continues to grow and the bodily organs mature until he or she is completely ready for life outside the womb. If the baby is born before the full term of pregnancy is complete, special care will probably be needed for the premature infant. Over half of children born in the seventh month survive (Fitch and Ratcliff 1991, 24).

Birth

It is not known what starts the birth process. The first stage of labor, lasting eight to 20 hours with the first child, involves the enlargement of the cervix through which the baby must pass to be born. The enlargement of the cervix occurs through contractions, which at first are mild and irregular, often about fifteen or twenty minutes apart and lasting one minute or less. With time they become more intense until they occur about two minutes apart. As a result of the contractions the cervix expands ("dilates") until it is ten centimeters wide and is large enough for the baby to pass through.

The second stage of birth involves the movement of the child through the cervix and into the outside world. This may take an hour or more with the first child. Generally the head is born first and then the remainder of the body. A few minutes later the mother expels the afterbirth, the third stage of birth.

Giving birth is hard work ("labor" is an apt term) and is painful—as God said it would be (Gen. 3:16). However, it can be a good experience or bad experience depending upon what you make of it. The expectations a mother has greatly influences how she will experience the birth. There are tribes in Africa that migrate from place to place to find food. If one of the women goes into labor while the tribe is migrating, she goes to the side of the road, squats down and has her baby, and then catches up with the rest of the tribe. In Europe, as in most of the world, women generally use natural childbirth, simply gritting their teeth during labor and enduring the pain rather than taking medications. Natural childbirth has also become popular with many American women. Research indicates that cultures that consider birth something to be hidden and fearful tend to have births that are long and difficult. In contrast, if birth is considered easy and open to others, brief and less problematic labor is more likely (Mead and Newton 1967). For this reason, Lamaze methods that minimize the expectation of pain, and a hospital birthing room that is open to the father and perhaps others, have proven to make birth a more positive experience for many families.

The boys were praying every night that mommy would have a baby girl. Don and Brenda were careful to tell them, after their prayers were finished, "But we'll love him just as much even if it's a boy." They wondered if the young faith of John and Stephen would be shaken if God blessed them with a son. But, deep within them, they too hoped for a girl. It would complete the family.

Brenda had been leaking water (amniotic fluid) all day, but the doctor was not encouraging. Two weeks overdue, and the baby was making momma very uncomfortable. "Will this baby ever be born?" they wondered as Don and Brenda tried to get to sleep. Suddenly, water came gushing out and they knew it was time to get to the hospital. Once at the hospital, Don and Brenda began several hours of walking up and down the hallways trying to encourage the baby's birth. Finally active labor began, and when she reached ten centimeters Brenda was told to push. After a number of exhausting contractions, the baby's head appeared. A squeeze bulb cleared the mouth and nose, and then the rest of the little one appeared. "It's a baby girl," the doctor said quietly. With tears in their eyes, Don asked, "Are you sure?" For years afterward the couple laughed about that question.

Mental Development

Can an unborn baby learn? Research (Spence and DeCasper 1982) has found that if mothers read a simple story to their unborn babies every day during the last three months of pregnancy, the baby shows a preference for that story shortly after birth. This does not, of course, indicate that the infant understands the story, but rather that they were able to recall (and preferred) the earlier sounds.

There is some relationship between birth weight and IQ (intelligence test) scores. However, there are many exceptions to this: some geniuses weigh only a few pounds at birth and some mentally retarded persons weigh quite a bit when born. If your child did not weigh much at birth, don't worry about it. If the child gains enough weight during the first six months of life there should be little effect on intelligence. To avoid low birth weight, expectant mothers should eat protein every day, drink some milk, take vitamin tablets with iron, and avoid things that can hurt the baby (see Chart 2-1).

Chart 2-1. Things to Avoid in Pregnancy

1. *Caffeine.* Several cups a day can endanger the child mentally and physically. Some doctors allow their pregnant patients a cup or two per day, but excessive use of caffeine has been linked to birth defects (Elan 1980). One researcher claims that the only safe amount is one-tenth of a cup each day!
2. *X-rays.* Because of the danger for the unborn baby, x-ray technicians use a special apron on every woman who is examined, just in case she is pregnant and does not know it. If the woman knows she is pregnant, it is best to avoid x-rays altogether.
3. *Drugs.* Many medications that are generally helpful to people become a great danger to the unborn child when the mother takes them. Even aspirins should not be taken without a doctor's approval. Illegal drugs are, of course, also extremely dangerous to the baby's health.
4. *Poor Nutrition.* During pregnancy don't go on a diet. While the mother should not overeat, as this can make the baby's delivery more difficult, it is important to get a good balance and adequate amount of the right foods so the child will not be physically deprived. A woman needs to gain at least 27 pounds during pregnancy to avoid having a low birth weight child (Fitch and Ratcliff 1991, 39). Most of that is gained during the last three or four months.
5. *Disease.* The mother should be extra careful during pregnancy to avoid being around others who have contagious diseases. Particularly dangerous are German measles and venereal diseases, as these can produce serious birth defects.
6. *Smoking.* Evidence is accumulating that smoking is dangerous to the unborn. Smaller babies and miscarriages have been associated with mothers smoking. Stillbirths, convulsions, and accelerated heartbeat in the newborn are also associated with the mother's smoking (Bolton 1983). There is evidence that children can be physically affected by either parent smoking after birth because the child must inhale some of the smoke.
7. *Alcohol.* Mothers who drink alcohol are likely to have a baby with "fetal alcohol syndrome," which involves physical abnor-

malities and retardation. Any amount of alcohol increases the likelihood of this syndrome.

8. *Stress.* A great deal of stress upon the mother can affect the unborn child because chemicals are released in the mother's body that can be passed on to the child, producing abnormalities such as cleft palate (Strean and Peer 1956), infant apathy (Newton and Newton 1962), and digestive disorders (Sontag 1941).
9. *Poisons.* Drinking contaminated water, breathing chemicals from certain sprays, or ingesting poison in some other manner, may result in the unborn child being poisoned.
10. *Anesthesia.* Lethargy has been noted in many babies born to mothers who received pain-killing medication during birth. Forceps delivery is also more likely. The least amount of anesthesia possible is the preferred amount.

Babies are born intelligent. A great deal of research in recent years shows that newborns can recall sights and sounds several seconds after they experience them and even relate those to new experiences (Freidman 1972). They are also motivated by immediate, repeated rewards for simple actions, such as sucking a nipple more than usual to make a mobile move.

Social, Emotional, and Personality Characteristics

What can parents do before the baby is born to assure good emotional and personality development? Nothing can absolutely guarantee health in this area, of course, but it is a good idea for you to work on both your marriage and relationship with *your* parents. This can help you avoid passing on unhealthy influences to your children from your marriage or family of birth. Read *Passages of Marriage* (Minirth, et al. 1991) with your spouse, and take the time to deal with the difficult areas from your past and present. Contact a counselor if you need more help. You'll have your hands full after the baby is born just caring for its needs!

Our advice to parents is that it is much better to wait awhile after marriage before having a baby. You need to be emotionally ready for children. Couples are more likely to get divorced if they have a child during the first two years of marriage than if they wait. It takes a couple of years merely to adjust to living with each other. If you have been married awhile and your marriage is floundering, the idea that having a baby will bring you closer together is nonsense. It will probably drive you farther apart. Work out your marital problems first; think about a family later.

From the moment of birth, babies have different personalities. Some cry a great deal, others cry very little. Some sleep quietly, others are restless in their sleep. Some are easier to sooth than others. There are cuddlers, but some babies do not want affection. However, sometimes some aspects of personality change as children develop. Activity level, for example, tends to be quite consistent throughout childhood (Walters 1965).

As noted in Chart 2-1, the mother receiving anesthesia during birth affects the newborn baby's activity level. While the effects on the baby's behavior are temporary, the first impressions by the parents are significantly affected. Mothers of these babies feed them less often, respond to them less, and show them less affection. Mothers report that these drugged babies were also harder to care for, and they related to them quite differently at two weeks of age (Osofsky and Connors 1979). Of course there are different degrees and kinds of anesthesia, and a bit of pain-killing medication just prior to birth may not affect the child at all.

Breast-Feeding

The newborn is best able to focus its eyes at a distance of nine inches, which is the distance between the baby and the mother's face during breast-feeding. Breast-feeding is better than bottle-feeding in many respects, especially during the early weeks of life. During the first few days, however, the baby does not get much milk from the mother because the infant doesn't need it. The fluid from the breast (colostrum) contains millions of maternal antibodies that help protect the child against infections. In addition, mother's milk contains proteins missing in other milk, as well as being sterile and inexpensive.

There is also an emotional warmth between the mother and baby during breast-feeding. Whether it promotes bonding or not is debatable. Breast-feeding does cause hormones to be released in the mother that cause the hips to pull back together, restoring her normal figure (Willson, Beecham, and Carrington, 1966, 613). These hormones also serve as a natural tranquilizer for the mother, encouraging feelings of acceptance toward the child (Lidz 1968, 130).

Research indicates that early infant feeding may help teach the baby to take turns (Kaye and Wells 1980). The pauses and bursts of sucking are thought to prepare the child for the taking of turns in conversation, thus aiding the long-term social development of the child.

It is important that breast-feeding not be accompanied by stress and tension. A relaxed approach will make the experience more pleasant for baby and mother alike. One study (McGrade 1968) indicates that babies who have a satisfactory breast-feeding experience as newborns (marked by high but unstressful activity after nipple withdrawal) are more active, happier, and less tense at eight months of age. Newborns that cried and thrashed upon nipple withdrawal were more tense and withdrawn by eight months. Nature has no more beautiful sight than a loving mother breast-feeding her totally dependent baby.

At this writing little Emma Beth is half past two. She gave up breast-feeding over a year ago. Brenda enjoyed the experience, and sometimes has deeply moving memories of her suckling baby daughter. While breast feeding is preferred, it is not always possible or desirable. A child is unlikely to be hurt emotionally if you choose to bottle feed. There was also a closeness for Brenda with their son Stephen, who could not be breast-fed because of a milk allergy.

As your baby gets older, be sure you don't overfeed. Extra fat cells made early in life may never be lost; if weight is lost later in life the extra cells only shrink but do not go away. As a result there can be a continual battle with being overweight throughout life. There may be danger in joining the "clean your plate" club.

Social Development

A number of research studies confirm the significance of the social relationship between the mother and child. Tape recordings of newborns were played to their mothers forty-eight hours after delivery. All of the mothers were able to select the cry of their own infants from more than thirty that were recorded (Formby 1967). This researcher also found that by the third night after birth each mother almost inevitably woke at the cry of her baby but not to the cry of other babies. These studies are a beautiful illustration of how strong mother-baby relationships can be.

Mothers become attached to their babies in a gradual sequence. Robson (1970, 976) found that until six weeks of age the average mother "experienced impersonal feelings of affection toward her infant, whom she tended to perceive as an anonymous nonsocial object." In the second month, when the infant began to smile and look at things longer, mothers reported stronger feelings of attachment and viewed the baby as a unique individual. After three months had passed, the absence of the infant resulted in unpleasant feelings by the mother and "his imagined loss an intolerable prospect" (Robson 1970, 976). In this study mothers who did not develop an attachment, or who developed it later than normal, generally did not want the baby or had babies with unusually negative behavior.

Children are not only developing a social relationship with the mother, they also have the rudiments of social relationships with others. Researchers have found that newborns can distinguish tape recordings of other infants crying from their own crying (Martin and Clark, 1982). They are also more likely to start crying when they hear other babies cry (Sagi and Hoffman 1976), possibly indicating the early development of feelings for others.

Ambivalence and Depression among Mothers

The emotional condition of the mother, both before and after birth of the child, is also an important consideration that may influence the child's development. Pregnancy, especially the first pregnancy, can be quite an anxiety-producing experience. *All women have ambivalent feelings about pregnancy when they are pregnant.* That is normal. The worst thing a pregnant woman can do is feel guilt about these ambivalent feelings or try to convince herself that she does not have them. If she keeps them pent up inside, they can cause physical changes in her body that can potentially damage her health as well as influence the physical and emotional development of the baby.

The best thing a pregnant woman can do is be aware of her ambivalence—such as the positive and negative aspects of having a baby and fears of the delivery—and talk them out with her husband and other significant people in her life. It is especially good to talk with another woman who has gone through the same experience. There is absolutely nothing abnormal or sinful about having these feelings. It would be abnormal if you did not have them. They will not do you any harm if you talk them out and resolve them. It is also important to have your emotional and spiritual needs met—have devotions every day, get plenty of rest, go out with your husband once a week or more, listen to relaxing Christian music, and continue having sexual intercourse as often as before pregnancy. Some medical textbooks recommend discontinuing sexual relations in the eighth month of pregnancy, while others indicate that sex can continue until delivery.

After the birth of the child it is not unusual for the mother to experience depression. If extreme, it is called "postpartum" (after-birth) depression. This serious form of depression begins soon after delivery and can last for months. Women with such extreme depression need antidepressant medications followed by long-term counseling sessions to help them accept motherhood.

On the other hand, most women feel somewhat let down after delivery. This is partly because they have lost some blood and are somewhat anemic. They also face getting up all hours of the night to change and feed the baby. But if the mother gets some help, eats right, and catches up on her sleep, the depression soon leaves. It also helps if the baby settles down to a more regular schedule in a few weeks. If the child does not develop a regular schedule by one or two months of age, it may be necessary to let the baby cry itself to sleep. Before you resort to this, be certain there are no physical problems that are involved.

Problems at Birth

Bill and Karen's (not their real names) second child was unusual. The infant needed a special feeding tube to eat, and seemed unusually lethargic. As months went by, they realized she was not developing like other children. At two years of age she still needed help to sit upright. At four she had not said her first word, and still could not eat solid food. It was clear that the youngster was severely retarded. While they occasionally shed tears about the difficulties, Bill and Karen came to accept the child as she was, and even took pride in the very small advancements she made. "Perhaps God gave her to us so we can more effectively minister to others who have children that are less than perfect," they concluded.

Difficulties can develop during pregnancy and at birth, producing birth defects in the newborn child. God has arranged a mother's physical body so that most fetuses with birth defects result in miscarriages during the first three or four months of pregnancy. The average mother will have about one miscarriage in every four or five pregnancies. But God allows some of these children with handicaps to be born.

There are a number of reasons for birth defects. Down's syndrome, for example, is a genetic problem producing unusual facial characteristics, a large tongue, and usually health problems. Most are mentally retarded to some degree. The mother drinking alcohol during pregnancy can cause fetal alcohol syndrome, resulting in slow growth, retardation, and deformities in various parts of the body. There are a number of possible physical causes for birth defects, many of which can be minimized by good prenatal care and following the guidelines in Chart 2-1.

Why does God allow birth defects? There are a number of possible reasons (Ratcliff 1980 and 1985b). Birth defects are the result of natural processes that are less than perfect because of the fall of humankind in the Garden of Eden. Because Adam and Eve sinned, both human nature and the natural world are now abnormal, different from what God intended. Birth defects are the result of our abnormal, fallen world, a side effect of human freedom. Yet God can sometimes use this abnormality for good—Francis Schaeffer and C. Everett Koop (1979) note that disabilities have the potential of bringing out compassion and caring from caretakers, characteristics that might not otherwise exist.

In the end, however, none of these explanations helps parents much because the problem is not as intellectual as it is emotional. Perhaps the best that can be done is to acknowledge that no one has the entire answer (Deut. 29:29) and affirm Romans 8:28: "And we know that in all things God works for the good of those who love him, who have been called according to his purpose."

One can expect parents to go through predictable stages of disbelief, anger toward God (or doctors, spouse, or others), anger toward self, and grief as they attempt to cope.

Hopefully the stages will conclude with resolution of the conflict, marked by greater maturity and understanding than before. Sometimes, however, parents can deny the problem completely or withdraw from others.

The families of children with birth defects must sometimes deal with placement and care issues as well. Is it better to try to help the child at home, find a special school, or place the child in a special facility? The answer is not always obvious, and we must be careful not to criticize a specific parent's decision. As Christians, we should do everything we can to help shoulder the burden of those who have children with birth defects (Ratcliff 1985b and 1990).

Spiritual Development

Tony and Adina prayed every night for their soon-to-be-born child. Sometimes Tony would lay his hands on the bulging tummy of his wife, fervently asking God to protect and guide their child both during the pregnancy and throughout life. After he was born, the couple affirmed their commitment by bringing the child forward in church for formal dedication.

The development of the child's spiritual life begins very early. At one time people thought that there need be little concern about such things until adolescence, or at the earliest during the school years, because the young child cannot understand theological abstractions. More recently, greater attention has been given to the earliest aspects of spiritual development, even in infancy (Ratcliff 1992a).

What has often been overlooked by parents and Christian educators is that spiritual development is not just a mental understanding of religion (such as reciting the Lord's prayer or making an affirmation of faith). While understanding is important, much of our later spiritual thinking and acting is built upon the early feelings, impressions, and experiences related to God, church, and our parents. For example, a person may have a difficult time trusting God because parents were inconsistent and unavailable during infancy. The mental, social, and emotional foundations laid by the parents, good or bad, can make it easier or harder for the child to have faith in God.

McDanald (1981), a Christian psychiatrist, believes he has traced some of his patients' spiritual and emotional difficulties to experiences in the womb. While this may seem far fetched at first glance, there is increasing evidence that the emotions felt by the mother influence the developing baby (David 1981). This influence occurs because of the chemical reactions of the mother that accompany traumatic events or other very negative emotional experiences. The chemical reactions in the mother can easily be transferred to the infant through the umbilical cord along with the nutrients from the mother. The result is a possible emotional influence that may affect the child throughout life, unless he or she receives counseling and therapy.

What can parents do to help the child spiritually during pregnancy and immediately after birth? The best spiritual foundation is good physical, mental, and emotional health. Guidelines for accomplishing these have been emphasized throughout this chapter. The mother should take care of herself emotionally and physically to give the baby every advantage spiritually. Spiritual development cannot be completely separated from other areas of development at any point of life, and especially in the earliest years.

An emotionally healthy home environment is just as important after the child is born. Both the mother and the father need to give the newborn the care that is needed. The presence of a lot of tension and discord may not be understood mentally by the infant, but can cause distress. Many researchers have found a link between the child's understanding of the parents and the understanding of God (Hyde 1990). This underscores the importance of a strong emotional bond between the parents and the child—those early feelings of attachment (or lack of attachment) very easily and unconsciously may transfer to God and spiritual faith. We have met numerous clients in our counseling experience who mentally want to have faith and confidence in Christ, but are emotionally troubled by long buried childhood and even infant experiences that keep them from vibrant spiritual living. We will examine the role of infant experiences upon spiritual development in greater detail in the next chapter.

Churches also have a role in helping the family with a newborn. The dedication of babies often includes promises to nurture the child spiritually, pledged by both the parents and members of the church congregation. What can the church do for newborns and their families?

We can help expectant and new parents by providing classes on the care of babies. These classes can encourage authoritative parenting of newborns (see chapter one), reading and discussing good books on parenting, and talking with experienced parents to learn from their experiences. Those in parenting classes should commit themselves to being good parents by drawing up specific guidelines they want to follow as parents. Teachers of such classes might help prospective parents imagine themselves in specific problem situations, so they can decide how they should respond. It may help to supplement the classes with hands-on experience with children, perhaps in the nursery, teaching Sunday school, or babysitting, and then reporting back to the class on what happened. We have driver training for teenagers, so why not training for prospective parents? Isn't being a good parent more important than being a good driver?

What else can churches do? Brenda and Don will never forget the kindness of church members who provided meals for the first few days after her release from the hospital. Those meals eased adjustment to life with their beloved newborn. The church can provide practical help such as counseling, understanding, and sometimes even financial help for parents of children with birth defects. Finally, the church should be sure that the quality of newborn care in the nursery is the very best possible, not just an afterthought.

The months of development before birth and the new presence of a baby in the house are an exciting time for many couples. I am the "Don" of Don and Brenda, and I would not trade anything for the joy and excitement of being present at the birth of all three of my children. The first author of this book shares in the excitement about birth; he enjoyed delivering babies more than any other experience during his medical school training. With the psalmist quoted at the beginning of this chapter, we too stand in wonder of God's "knitting."

3

Babies and Toddlers

Emma Beth, now two and one-half years old, has drastically changed since she was born. She grew from a helpless little baby, who even needed her head supported, to the young girl who cannot imagine why you would walk when you can run. She once loved to be cuddled all day long, but now only cuddles when she first wakes up—the rest of the time she is constantly occupied with other things. The helpless infant could only cry to help us guess what was wrong, our toddler not only tells us what she wants but keeps up a running dialogue on everything all day long. She tripled her weight in two years (let's hope that never happens again!) and should weigh 30 to 35 pounds by her third birthday.

Of course not all children develop at the same rate. Sickness that lasts over several weeks can slow down growth, although after they get well these children grow faster to make up for lost time. There are wide variations in normal growth rates. By the way, there is almost no relationship between the speed or amount of physical growth and eventual intelligence.

Dr. Lidz (1968, 117) at Yale University comments that life changes more during infancy than at any other time. If parents fail to provide proper physical care, the child will suffer with ill health, perhaps for the rest of life. It is especially important to beware of dehydration, in which the baby loses water through vomiting or diarrhea—severe dehydration requires immediate hospitalization or the child may die. Social interaction during infancy and toddlerhood is also important; neglect in this area will result in emotional problems and inadequate intellectual growth.

An improper diet can influence the infant's intellectual capacity, since all of the brain cells a person will ever have are produced by six months of age (Ziai 1969, 48). After six months of age brain cells may enlarge but no more new cells will ever be formed. This is why the infant needs plenty of protein, primarily from milk, during those first six months. Some mothers in poverty feed their babies Kool-Aid because they cannot afford much milk. The result is fewer brain cells for their children for the rest of their lives. Even programs like Head Start cannot make up for these kinds of deficiencies because they come too late. How much better it would be if they would breast-feed them! Satisfying physical needs is extremely important during infancy and toddlerhood.

Mental Development

Jean Piaget (1950), the famous Swiss researcher, described the infant as being in the sensory-motor stage of development. This is because the baby gains so much ability in using the senses (hearing, seeing, tasting, touching, etc.) and learns so many motor skills (crawling, walking, and so on).

During the first month, the baby learns by repeating the reflexes with which he or she is born, such as sucking, crying, blinking, and breathing. During the second month, the infant learns that he or she can control some of these activities. The baby sticks the thumb in the mouth, stares, sucks, and makes noises at will. During the next few months play, imitation, and investigation of objects with the mouth and hands begin. Before long children start crawling, and babies often begin walking by the end of the first year. He or she tries to directly experience everything available because this is the only way of learning at this age.

To deal with the natural and desirable interest in everything within reach, parents should childproof the house. The average American home contains many poisons and medications that an exploring infant could get into, such as furniture polish, aspirins, and insecticides. The major cause of death in infancy is accidents, often because children investigate these dangerous things. Yet infants who grow up in homes where they are constantly getting their hands slapped for investigating tend to become adults who are rigid in their thinking and fearful of exploring new ideas. We personally know of one infant who died from drinking furniture polish when he was supposed to be napping. It can happen to anyone.

The average one-year-old can say about one or two words, like "dada" and "momma." Some can say a few more words than this while others do not start speaking until several months later. The rate of speech development does not predict the amount of intelligence the child will eventually have, unless the infant is very far behind. Do not push your infant—accept and enjoy the child as he or she is. Even Albert Einstein was said to be a late developer. Just give the child a wide range of experiences, and he or she will move on to the next stage when physically ready to do so.

The toddler is in the second stage of mental development, according to Piaget, when he or she learns that words stand for objects and actions. During infancy most children babble a great deal. Even at six months of age they understand the tones of language, as well as the natural rhythms of speech (Kaplan and Kaplan 1971). At the beginning of the toddler stage, about fifteen months of age, most children are using single words to name some familiar things such as "mommy," "daddy," "dog," and "eat." They combine such words with babbling until they start putting two or more words together, usually at about eighteen to twenty-four months of age. The average child can talk in sentences fairly well by three years of age, which marks the end of the toddler stage. Language development depends a good deal on how much parents talk to the child, as well as whether he or she has older brothers and sisters to learn from. Parents should encourage their child's speech by listening to their sometimes halting statements, and restating words and phrases that are unclear (do this without scolding or criticism). Toddlers learn to think out loud by talking to themselves, which is perfectly normal.

Yet toddlers are also very self-centered, believing that the whole world revolves around them. An eighteen-month-old's logic consists primarily of impulses to carry out selfish desires. He or she cannot think ahead to the future and thinks primarily of the present, frequently forgetting the lessons learned from recent experiences. Some adults in today's society still appear to be operating with the logic of the toddler! Gradually, children surrounded by a healthy family environment learn that the universe does not revolve around them. They learn that they are important to God, even though they are not the center of everyone's attention. As the psalmist stated:

> When I consider your heavens,
> the work of your fingers,
> the moon and the stars,
> which you have set in place,

what is man that you are mindful of him,
the son of man that you care for him?
You made him a little lower than the heavenly beings,
and crowned him with glory and honor.

Psalm 8:3–5

Social and Emotional Characteristics

Socialization and affection are just as important as physical needs for the infant and toddler. As noted in the last chapter, the ability to trust develops during infancy. At this time they will either become basically trusting of others or basically distrustful. What makes the difference? The answer is how trustworthy the parents are in meeting the child's basic needs (Erikson 1963). The baby is among the most helpless and dependent of all God's creatures, and without enough support the infant will struggle for emotional survival. Later, during toddlerhood, too much support can lead the infant to be overly dependent. At that point the parents must strike a balance between too much and too little support.

The Need for Stimulation

During World War II, many European infants were placed in foundling homes due to the death or disappearance of their parents. They were cared for by nurses at a ratio of one adult for every eight to twelve babies. They were fed well and received good medical attention, but received very little stimulation because the nurses were so busy. As a result of this lack of stimulation 30 percent of them died of malnutrition within the first year. Most of those who survived could not stand, walk, or talk by the age of four, and had become permanently and severely mentally retarded (Spitz 1945). This condition in which the infant refuses to eat and literally starves itself to death is known as *marasmus,* also called "failure to thrive."

Marasmus also exists in the United States, generally in homes where parents are physically abusive or where the father is an alcoholic. Sometimes these babies must be legally taken out of their homes and placed in foster homes, either permanently, or until their parents learn to take care of their children. But if caught in time, and given a lot of physical stimulation, some of these infants recover and live fairly normal lives afterward (Evans 1972).

Paul Meier knew of a very small, thin six-year-old boy who illustrates the result of little stimulation. As a baby, his mother worked long hours and left him daily with his grandmother. Unfortunately, the grandmother could not tolerate children, so she put him in a crib in front of a TV every day. The television was in a small room with nothing and no one else in it; the TV was his sole companion. Throughout the day his only human contact was when his grandmother brought in food and laid it in the crib. By age six he was the size of an average three-year-old and could not talk except for repeating TV commercials, which he did over and over again. When asked questions, he would spout off some TV commercial quite accurately. While a number of people at the psychiatric hospital tried to help him, he was permanently injured physically and mentally. After his mother received some training, he was returned to her custody.

This "TV Kid" is an extreme example of the widespread neglect of children that is more common than many of us would like to think. Young children can be seen playing outside much of the night in some inner city areas, and even if they are inside, they get little attention. We weep for them.

What are some other effects of little stimulation of infants? Perhaps some research with animals can give us some clues. Puppies who were restricted to cages developed very unusual behavior when they grew up. When allowed to leave their cages, they became overly excited by anything new in their environment. They began to whirl so violently that they would skin their heads against nearby walls. They also ran around the room, going from object to object but failing to pay very much attention to anything for long. These deprived dogs also had great difficulty getting along with normally reared dogs that were near them (Melzack 1969). Perhaps this suggests that hyperactivity and poor social relationships can sometimes be related to lack of stimulation and neglect during early childhood. Without question, people—like animals—are powerfully affected by the amount and type of stimulation received in infancy. Many other studies also show this fact (see Hall, Lamb, and Perlmutter 1986, 193–94).

Mother Substitutes

Can anyone take mother's place? Thirty or forty years ago the question would have seemed crazy, but today many seem to feel that the mother's role is not all that important. At present about half of mothers go back to work before the baby is one year old. About 45 percent of these youngsters are cared for by relatives other than parents and about the same percentage stay in private homes that offer day care. During the second year, only 28 percent are with relatives, while nearly 20 percent move into group care (day-care homes stay at 45 percent). Group care escalates even further during the third year (Bachrack, Hown, Mosher, and Simizu 1985).

What are the effects of mother-absent care of infants? Most of the studies that show no problems (and sometimes positive results for deprived children) are conducted in extremely high quality centers run by university researchers. These nearly perfect situations are a far cry from typical day-care homes and centers in the United States, where staff are underpaid and there is little individual attention for babies. Not only is disease much more likely when babies are in day care (Farnan 1989), but Belsky (1988, Steinburg and Belsky 1991) shows that they are more aggressive, disobedient, withdrawn, and not as attached to parents. These tendencies last at least into the school years, when they also get lower grades.

While it may be unpopular to say this in our modern era, infants need at least one consistently available person for security and socialization, or there will probably be some kind of permanent emotional and intellectual damage. For most families this would be the mother (natural or adoptive).

We strongly advise those of you who are married working mothers, especially if you have a baby, to quit your jobs. Don't be afraid to deprive your children of material things if you can give them your time instead. Personal, loving attention is far more important than having the latest and fanciest clothes and toys.

As in infancy, mother substitutes during the toddler years present a serious problem. Any prolonged separation from the mother during this stage can result in a loss of initiative or even the determination to survive. Many children in the United States are being farmed out to day-care centers, many of which are very detrimental to the child's mental health. High quality day care, with adequate staff and good materials for learning, possibly may be beneficial for underprivileged children. But good day care is usually so expensive that it does not pay for the mother to work outside the home.

What makes for high quality day care? Some researchers suggest that there be at least one teacher for every three children. Second, the adults need to talk to each child a great deal (Belsky 1988, Hall, Lamb, and Perlmutter 1986, 414). Third, care must be taken to minimize the spread of disease. In other words, the best day care is as much like a good home as possible. We are sure few day-care centers can accomplish even these three guidelines consistently. Why not simply stay home and be sure your child gets what is needed? If you are a single parent, perhaps a relative can take on the parent role while you work, but this is clearly a second-best alternative to parental care.

The importance of the parent staying home was emphasized in a study of prisoners that was done by distinguished London psychiatrists (Brown 1966, 1048). They concluded that the main factors contributing to the criminal behavior of the prisoners were "multiplicity of care and lack of stable parent figures in childhood." Fathers are also important to young children. Another study showed that boys whose fathers were not present for a considerable amount of time during toddlerhood and the preschool years had "more anti-social behavior than those whose father [were] consistently present" (McCandless 1967, 173). Either father or mother absence has many negative results on children (Hall, Lamb, and Perlmutter 1986, 416–19; Youst 1992, 23–30).

Ideally, toddlers should have their mothers home with them during the day, and both parents home to interact with during evenings and weekends. The high divorce rate in America is separating children from their fathers, and in most cases the mothers are forced by economics to go to work, so children are deprived of a stable relationship with their mothers. The psychological toll on children of divorced parents is enormous, and lasts for many years, as we will see later in this book. God's Word says, "Therefore, what God has joined together, let man not separate" (Mark 10:9).

If a child loses one or both parents through death, it is time for grandparents, other close relatives, or close friends to step in and help the toddler reestablish a close mother- or father-child relationship as soon as possible, even if the close relative or friend does not live in the same house. Children need two parents! In these circumstances, the surviving parent should seriously consider remarriage to a stable Christian person. As the Apostle Paul stated, "I counsel younger widows to marry, to have children, to manage their homes and to give the enemy no opportunity for slander" (1 Tim. 5:14).

Relating to Other Children

By two years of age, the toddler should begin to develop relationships with other children. If the child has been able to trust the parents, he or she should be able to express and assert the self with others, even though sometimes this will be a bit crude at first. With encouragement and correction by parents and other adults, the toddler will begin to develop social skills (junior church can also be a place to work on social skills at this age). The presence of other children after the second birthday is very important because the toddler is emotionally ready to learn social skills by this age. This does not mean the child needs to be in day care all day, which is too much for most toddlers. But an hour or two each week with other children, supervised with one or more trustworthy adults, can be a good experience.

I was once contacted about a five-year-old who could not adjust to school. As I spoke to the parents it became apparent that he had never been around other children! The parents had no neighbors or relatives with children, and the boy had accompanied the parents to adult Sunday school and church all his life. It was no wonder that he was terrified by a room of active five-year-olds! I suggested that the parents take the child out of school and gradually expose him to a few children for a couple of hours each day. After a few weeks he had developed enough social skills to attend school. How much better it would have been if he had gained those skills as a toddler!

One important social skill is especially important: sharing. The foundation for unselfishness, generosity, and not stealing is laid during the toddler stage. Our children have lots of sibling rivalry just like other children, but they also share because we praise them whenever they share with each other or with us. We try to set the example by sharing many of our things with them. When a toddler takes a toy out of another's hands, we slap the child's hand or spank. This is stealing, in a primitive sort of way. It is not too early to teach the toddler that coveting a neighbor's possessions is wrong.

Toddlers sometimes develop imaginary friends that they talk to. This is normal. Their fantasy life helps them practice talking and also helps them deal with conflicts they are experiencing in ways that are less threatening than real life.

Sit back and watch your children play house. It is quite revealing to see how our children interpret family activities and communication. In fact, many child psychiatrists do just that—it is called play therapy—to analyze what is going on in the family and is causing the child's conflicts. They use the information to help the child and the parents to resolve those conflicts. By watching the children play, parents may be able to see misunderstandings and potential problems, and either correct the child or correct their own actions as needed. It is also great fun to see their recreations of family life!

Pacifiers and Thumb-Sucking

Mothers frequently ask about pacifiers and thumb-sucking. We think pacifiers are fine, although they can be dangerous if the parent ties them around the neck of the infant or toddler. While this keeps the pacifier from getting lost, the child could fall, catch the string on something, and choke. Also, worn-out pacifiers should be thrown away and replaced, because the rubber end of the pacifier can break loose and choke a toddler who bites through it.

However, infants and toddlers generally need a good deal of sucking and other mouth activity. Children who suck on a pacifier as much as they want during infancy and the first half of the toddler stage generally do not suck their thumbs as much when they leave these stages. We have found this to be the case with our children, and we both have had children who refused pacifiers completely, even in infancy.

If your children suck their thumbs, the best advice we can give is not to worry about it—this is quite normal. Babies even suck their thumbs in the womb! Just ignore thumb-sucking and it will probably stop when they enter school, because of the teasing of other children. Some parents are afraid that thumb-sucking will result in buck teeth, but research (Ziai 1969) indicates this is rarely the case. About 20 percent still suck their thumbs even after their sixth birthday (Freedman and Kaplan 1967, 1383). If an older child is sucking the thumb because of anxiety, family counseling might be considered.

Personality Development

By the time the child is old enough to go to school, most of the personality and character is established. An emotionally healthy, reflective child will be greatly enriched by his new contact with teachers, other children, and studies. However, if the roots of anxiety are laid in infancy through lack of acceptance, the child is more likely to fear the unknown and feel threatened by school.

Mothers need to be unconditionally accepting of their babies if the baby is later to have healthy self-acceptance, a good conscience, and a belief that he or she is relatively free (McDanald 1967, 74). On the other hand, if the baby is only loved part of the time (such as only when quiet), undue anxiety, guilt, and hostility are more likely, which can produce compulsive or antisocial actions. In other words, if babies are not given a lot of attention and affection, they may become overly concerned with being perfect as adults, or possibly have little or no conscience.

Many years ago Harry and Margaret Harlow (1965), a husband and wife team, did interesting research that also shows how important affection is. They took a group of young monkeys away from their mothers and made them choose between two imitation mothers. One "mother" was made of wire and had a baby bottle attached that was kept full of milk. The other "mother" was a soft, terry cloth mother, but with no milk bottle. The monkeys would get milk from the wire mother, but ran to the soft terry cloth mother whenever they were frightened. The soft touch and constant, loving care is crucial in infancy. Be a soft terry cloth mother, not a wire mother!

Once the child becomes a toddler, at about fifteen months, it is possible to meet his or her desires too much. Overly indulged toddlers may become too optimistic and expect the world to give them their every wish, as their parents did when they were youngsters. They may give up quickly when success does not come immediately. Parents must not become overly concerned about the effects of minor stresses on babies and toddlers. Psychological trauma and deprivation are never desirable, but some natural stress can be beneficial. Lidz (1968, 88) notes that overprotection in early life is more likely to produce "colorless individuals," while the presence of some difficulty can strengthen the personality.

Toddlerhood is a crucial stage in the development of basic self-trust and self-confidence. A domineering, overdemanding, overprotective mother will develop in her toddler a lack of self-trust, self-worth, and initiative. A sense of worthlessness results from constantly not living up to parental expectations. While discipline is needed (as will be emphasized shortly), it must never be at the expense of self-worth. The parents need to recognize and praise positive, self-controlled behavior.

Sometimes parents get into the trap of seeing their child as an extension of the self, expecting him or her to complete parents' lives by living out the life they did not or could not live. This sometimes leads to overdependence and limiting the child's self-direction and independence. When the mother does this, and the husband is absent or quite passive, it can help create severe psychological problems for the child (Lidz 1972). Overprotection is a dangerous threat to healthy personality development.

Heredity or Environment?

Debates have gone on for years questioning whether heredity (genetics and other biological factors one is born with) or the environment (everyday events) influence the child the most. Two generations ago there was an overemphasis on heredity. People believed that a person was a criminal because of an inherited criminal mind, a head that was shaped like a criminal, and similar foolishness. Someone once said, "heredity is what a man believes in until his son begins to behave like a delinquent."

Then came a generation that blamed nearly everything on the environment and ignored heredity. Personality was thought to be purely the result of the rewards and punishments that parents provided. Today we know that there is some truth in both ideas. Babies are born with different dispositions, as mentioned in the last chapter. For example, children have an inherited activity level. Most boys are more active than most girls because they have a higher level of androgen in their blood. However, basic dispositions can be encouraged or discouraged. They can be shaped and developed to some extent by the experiences kids have in childhood, especially early childhood. As we will see in the section on spiritual development, the heredity versus environment question affects how we see the spiritual nature of the child as well.

Birth Order and Child Roles

Does birth order make a difference in personality development? While this idea has probably been exaggerated, and we must allow for many exceptions to the rules, there are some general personality trends observed according to order of birth. Older children are more likely to have demands placed on them, so often they become perfectionists. As adults they are more likely to achieve success, but enjoy it less while wishing they could have done more. Second children are sometimes more shy and polite, trying to please everyone. They may arbitrate differences between the other children. Subsequent children are often more outgoing and enjoy life more than the firstborn, but also are less successful. The youngest child is more likely to be indulged and thus may become selfish, dependent, and less mature.

I can recall how my children came to have some of the above trends. With my oldest son, his mother and I—like many new parents—were concerned that John develop normally and do well. Really we were too concerned. When he was nine or ten months old but still not walking, we began to wonder if he was okay. Over and over again, we encouraged him to take his first steps. On his first birthday he took off walking on his own, with little help from us. As he neared age two we wondered why he was not talking more. Was there a problem? We worked and worked on helping him say words. Then the speech part of his brain kicked in and he has not stopped talking since (unlike many boys, he is extremely verbal, something that often goes with being left-handed). These are just a few examples of the many times we pushed him to do well. Perhaps the extra pushing was because he was the only child taking our attention! Today, as a ten-year-old, John is extremely bright, but also a perfectionist with himself and others. Our second son, Stephen, received a more relaxed parenting approach. After all, we had learned how to do it with John, and now two children took our time and attention. We had also learned that IQ does not relate very much to physical development. We let him be a child. He seems to enjoy life more than his older brother, and is very social. But Stephen is also an exception to the trends, as he does not fit the other characteristics of secondborn children. And we are purposefully trying to avoid indulging Emma Beth, so she will not fit the pattern for youngest children. But we must admit it is hard, especially since she is the only girl! Parents can make the difference in whether a particular child will fit the birth order trends or be an exception. Birth order effects are clearly learned, because kids are treated differently, not the result of heredity. Perhaps that explains why there are so many exceptions to the trends.

Sometimes children take on special roles within the family, regardless of birth order, such as scapegoat, baby, pet, miniature husband or wife, and peacemaker. Most of these roles are harmful and to be avoided. Another tendency is for children of older parents to be more serious minded than children of young parents.

Twins

About one in eighty-nine births produces twins, and about one-third of these are identical twins. Older mothers are more likely to have twins (Schichedanz, Hansen, and Forsyth, 1990, 74–75). We think twins are a special blessing from the Lord. But having twins also gives parents added responsibility. The American tradition is to dress twins alike and have them do everything alike. But studies have shown that this is not the best thing for them psychologically (Freedman and Kaplan 1967, 1493). It's best to deal with them as separate individuals. Respect differences in their tastes and opinions. Don't reward, praise, or punish them at the same time, but do so individually. It is better if they wear different styles of clothing, depending on their own tastes. It is even recommended that they attend different classes in school.

Discipline

Discipline should be kept to a minimum during the first year of life. If the areas where the baby plays have been adequately baby-proofed, there will not be much need for discipline. At about eight or nine months of age parents may begin saying "no" as they pull the baby away from forbidden objects. This will need to be repeated many times for most children. After ten or fifteen times of saying "no" and pulling away the child, some parents may wonder if they have a slow learner on their hands, but this is simply the normal way children learn at this age.

Sometime after the first birthday babies learn that they too can say "no!" This is the beginning of what James Dobson (1970) terms "willful defiance," where the child challenges parental authority. He or she is saying (by tone of voice, if not using these actual words), "Oh yeah? Who's gonna make me?" The child is wanting to know who is boss, and the parent needs to let him know the answer.

Dr. Dobson makes a distinction between willful defiance and childish irresponsibility. All children are irresponsible at times, simply forgetting to do what is asked or accidentally spilling the milk at dinner. Spanking is completely inappropriate for irresponsible behavior. Cleaning up the mess or not being allowed to play for a few minutes are more appropriate reactions to these situations. Punishment using physical contact should be reserved for those (hopefully) rare situations where the child is clearly calling into question the parent's right to be in charge.

At first the punishment for defiance will be a slap on the hand. Dobson (1978, 46) recommends that this not be done prior to fifteen months of age. We suggest that this not be a hard and fast rule—children become openly defiant at different ages. Slapping before the first birthday is always inappropriate, and there are perhaps some children who never become defiant—although neither of us have such a child in our families!

We do not believe in child abuse in any form. Punishment by striking a child is dangerous for some parents whose anger can make them hit harder than they intended. A good rule of thumb is: if the striking leaves a mark, it was too hard. Yet if the child does not cry, it probably was not hard enough. One thump on the hand is usually enough at this age.

The Bible makes clear that discipline is central to childrearing. Consider these passages:

> He who spares the rod hates his son,
> but he who loves him is careful to discipline him.
>
> (Prov. 13:24)

> Discipline your son, for in that there is hope.
>
> (Prov. 19:18)

> Folly is bound up in the heart of a child,
> but the rod of discipline will drive it far from him.
>
> (Prov. 22:15)

> Do not withhold discipline from a child;
> if you punish him with the rod, he will not die.
> Punish him with the rod
> and save his soul from death.
>
> (Prov. 23:13–14)

> The rod of correction imparts wisdom,
> but a child left to himself disgraces his mother.
>
> (Prov. 29:15)

> Discipline your son, and he will give you peace;
> he will bring delight to your soul.
>
> (Prov. 29:17)

These verses are especially relevant for rearing the two- and three-year-old, for it is then that the need for discipline really blossoms. Toddlerhood is one of the most trying stages for parents because the child is curious about everything you call a "no-no." By removing many of these "no-nos," the youngster can still be allowed and even encouraged to follow the natural bent toward exploration. During the first fifteen months of life parents should encourage the child to be as independent as possible. But during the next twenty-one months or so, the toddler stage, they must teach the child to respect limits and not give in to the immediate desires. Of course the parents should still encourage a healthy degree of independence.

Paul Meier and his wife were very loving and nurturing parents. "Yet we remember spanking our older son or slapping his hands for open rebellion (sometimes repeatedly) during that crucial time between fifteen months of age and the third birthday. By encouraging independence and exploration, yet spanking him for willful disobedience, he came out of the experience well-behaved for his age. On the other hand, he continued to have a healthy degree of independence at the same time. Some children rebel beyond their third birthday, but for our oldest son that birthday brought on a new era of relative peace—although he still needed an occasional spanking. As he grew older he tried hard to please us, doing his chores and going to bed when asked without complaining, and he rarely needed more than a sad or scornful look to correct his behavior. We kept the paddle handy though. In addition, the younger children were easier to discipline than he was, because they followed his good example." Of course, some children are more obstinate and willful than others, seemingly from birth, but consistent predictable discipline usually keeps the defiance to a minimum.

In disciplining the child and setting firm limits, which is absolutely necessary, parents must also be realistic as to what is expected in a child at this age. Parents are still learning what can realistically be expected of a child when rearing their first-born. As noted earlier, many of them become quite perfectionistic because their parents expected too much of them as they grew up.

We as parents are frequently very disappointed when we have just spanked our child for getting into something forbidden, only to find the youngster doing it again five minutes later. The right thing to do, in our opinion, is to patiently spank him or her again, rather than to throw up our hands and scream. Children at the toddler stage have very short attention spans and short memories. They are also unlikely to understand complex reasoning, which is a waste of time at this age. Verbal reproofs are sometimes adequate, but if the child is openly rebelling, spanking is more effective. Parents should be aware of these age characteristics, and realize that the dos and don'ts may need to be repeated many times before a toddler understands them. Although the behavior of the toddler may become exasperating, especially when it results in the destruction of some precious object, or in a mess that takes time to clean up, what the child really needs at this stage of life is calm parents.

Sometimes parents get into the habit of yelling at their children. This is a very unhealthy characteristic, as it threatens the child's self-esteem and self-worth. As James Dobson has sometimes commented, even good parents can become screamers because the loudness scares the child (at least the first few times) and temporarily stops them. Before long it takes a yet louder and louder noise to stop them until yelling at the child becomes a way of life. It is far healthier for parent and child alike to stop the screaming and simply back up threats with action. Quietly and calmly tell children what punishment will come if they disobey, and then follow up on your promise. A single, gentle warning is enough. Screaming is unnecessary.

Discipline, as well as the general care of children, is made far more difficult today because the average family is separated from grandparents and other extended family members. With one family in four moving each year, there are fewer relatives to talk with and help care for the children. Books and television programs often provide confusing and conflicting advice (Collins 1971, 4).

One of the results is that parents frequently make mountains out of molehills, worrying about things that are absolutely normal—especially with the first child. For example, thumb-sucking, genital play, and security objects (blankets, teddy bears, etc.) are all normal ways in which youngsters gain comfort.

The Bible emphasizes that children learn morality and wisdom through discipline. Young children often imitate and try to please their parents to avoid punishment for being bad, and to gain approval for being good.

Typical Problems

Crying

What can be done for a crying baby? The key, of course, is to find what causes the crying. The source of discomfort can be anything from pain to boredom. Here are a few suggestions for comforting a crying baby:

1. Feeding the child food or milk.
2. Increasing or decreasing temperature by adding or removing clothing.
3. Singing or talking to the child.
4. Burping the child to remove gas bubbles.
5. Rubbing or touching the baby with a soft object or with your skin (sometimes holding tightly will help).
6. Rocking the child.
7. Changing the position of the child, carrying the baby.
8. Playing a tape with pulsing sounds or soothing music.
9. Applying medication for teething pain or supplying teething toys.
10. Changing the diaper.

Sometimes what the crying child needs most is sleep. Unfortunately, they do not always realize this and so even good babies may need to cry themselves to sleep from time to time. This does not hurt the child, in fact some believe it helps them give the lungs needed exercise. By the way, a baby needs about sixteen to eighteen hours of sleep every twenty-four hours.

Can a crying baby simply be manipulating the parents for attention or to get its way? While this is certainly possible after about six months of age, it is unlikely before that point. It is generally wise to try to find the cause of the crying, and babies whose mothers quickly respond to their cries generally cry far less than other children (Ainsworth, Bell, and Slayton 1972). If crying is persistent, consult a doctor.

Toilet Training

Potty training the toddler can sometimes produce emotional problems that can last throughout life. It can be rough on the child too! Parents who try to toilet train their infants in the first year of life are attempting something that is biologically impossible. The nerves that signal the need for the potty do not mature until after eighteen months of age, and sometimes they are not ready until age four or more. To train a child before he or she is biologically ready is to invite extreme frustration for parent and child alike, and possibly contribute to long-term psychological problems.

How can you know if the child is ready for potty training? An interest in the topic is a cue. Certainly if the toddler can tell you they are going in the diaper, they are ready for training. It is a real help in training if the child has developed a fairly regular schedule of toileting.

Use rewards and not punishment in toilet training. Place the toddler on the potty—a special small stool for the child will be less frightening—and explain that they will get a favorite reward (candy, stickers, etc.) when they go in the potty. Give them lots of pop or other favorite drinks as they sit, as well as some activities to keep them occupied. You might show them what you want by using a doll that wets itself.

If only by accident, children should be successful eventually. Immediately praise them and give them the reward. Be sure to tell them the name of what they did using whatever term you decide is appropriate. Don't be afraid to show your excitement at the child's success. The rewards will give them motivation to repeat the toileting—but don't give too much of the reward or it will wear out quickly. If the reward no longer motivates, find a new reward that does. You might even let your child choose from several alternative rewards. Also do not give the reward at any time other than when they are successful. I have known parents who even put Cheerios in the stool to encourage toileting—boys enjoy target practicing! If the child has accidents, correct by saying something like "no M & M's for you, you didn't go in the potty," but don't spank. You might, however, have them clean up any mess that is made (if they don't want to do this, you can put your hands over theirs as you help them clean it up).

Eventually they will learn the terms for what they need to do, and they will use those terms when they need to toilet. Do not delay taking them to the potty, and of course continue to use the rewards with each success. After they have regular successes, you can begin teaching the child to wipe and pull the pants up and down. Once these have been learned, rewards can be gradually phased out. After a week or so of regular success, give them praise every time, but only give the reward every other time. A week or so later give them a reward every third time, then after another week give them a treat only occasionally for success. Eventually just give them praise.

Food Refusal

Refusing to eat is common during the late toddler stage. This is frequently a way of manipulating to express hostility toward a parent. But sometimes toddlers simply do not like certain foods. The oldest son of Paul Meier went through a stage of not liking meat when he was about two years old. "He would eat everything else on his plate and leave the meat. We knew it was important for him to eat protein, so I asked a nutritionist at the medical center where I worked what she would recommend. She gave me such a simple solution I was almost embarrassed for asking. She told me to put protein and nothing else on his plate for a few days. If he did not eat protein, he would not eat. When he got hungry enough he would get used to eating meat. It worked beautifully and took only one or two meals to break him in." Don't let your toddler succeed in getting you angry by refusing to eat—just remove the food if he or she becomes too negative or dawdles too much. It will not hurt the child to miss a meal or two occasionally—in fact it will help in the long run. Do not give the toddler any between meal snacks unless the child has earned that right by eating a reasonable amount at the previous mealtime. Meals should be a time for developing social skills, especially between parents and toddler, as well as a time for eating. Be sure you do not substitute food for love or social interaction.

Sexuality

We recommend that you ignore genital play during the infant and toddler stages, unless your child is doing so in public. It is part of the natural exploration involved in discovering the body. If you choose not to ignore it, handle the situation tactfully by merely putting the underwear or diaper back on and telling the child to leave it on. But do not ever shame the child for it, or threaten him or her in any way, or the child may think the genitals are evil and develop poor sexual concepts later in life. This might even result in sexual fears or impotence as an adult.

When children ask questions about their bodies, and they usually do either at this stage or during the preschool years, give them truthful, matter-of-fact answers. It is generally felt best to use correct words such as vagina and penis rather than childish terms. Some parents easily become embarrassed when asked about such matters, and perhaps the parent who feels least self-conscious should do most of the explaining. It may help parents to practice by role-playing the discussion with one another. Be sure you only answer the question being asked; it is more natural for children to learn about sexuality bit by bit than by having a long, detailed description of the whole topic.

Fears and Handicaps

Sometimes a fear of strangers develops toward the end of the first year, and sometimes a fear of animals develops as well. By the preschool years animal fears are the most common. Some children fear a large body of water and become anxious when they see the seashore for the first time, not wanting to wade into ankle deep waves. Fear of heights is probably learned by early experiences, such as falling off the couch a couple of times!

Fears are sometimes desirable. A fear of climbing a thirty foot tree may be very desirable for a three-year-old! Fears may also tell you that something needs to be corrected. My three-year-old son once displayed an extreme fear of church. He would begin crying whenever the building came into view. The source of his fear was discovered when my wife observed the five-year-olds in his junior church class regularly hitting the younger children. Likewise, fear of a certain individual may possibly indicate that they have experienced pain or abuse by that person. Always try to understand the source of a fear before attempting to change it.

What can be done about fears? If a fear is unhealthy, it is a good idea to gradually expose children to the feared object, while giving them comfort. Begin by just being in the same room with the object, while holding them and talking quietly about the feared person or thing. As they become relaxed, you can move a bit closer to the feared object. Eventually, if you do this gradually enough, they should get over their fears. Extreme fears often require help from a counselor.

If you have a handicapped child, they need special attention. Even more than nonhandicapped children, they require their mother's unconditional love and acceptance to prepare them for what they will face when they are old enough to go to school. If staying at home with their children is important for mothers in general, it is doubly important for the handicapped. Hospitalized children also need their mothers. Studies have shown that young children whose mothers do not come and spend a lot of time with them in the hospital have a significantly higher death rate (Lidz 1968, 150; and Lynch, Steinberg, and Ounsted 1975).

Spiritual Development

In the previous section on heredity and environment, we mentioned that most specialists in child development now believe that both are important. What people think on this issue also affects how they look at the child spiritually.

For example, when Paul Meier was at Duke University Medical Center he heard a liberal theologian who taught that "children are born princes and princesses, and the environment makes frogs out of them" (Barnes 1974). He said that children are born with a good nature, rather than a sinful nature, and that their parents teach them disobedience. If this were the whole story, then our children must have missed some of the genes they were supposed to receive—they were disobeying before they learned to talk!

The Bible does emphasize that we are created in God's image (Gen. 1:26–27) so there is something wonderful and beautiful about children. Even more conservative theologians support the idea of a positive aspect to human nature, calling it "common" or "prevenient" grace. But the Bible also emphasizes the fact that the image of God is badly scarred in human nature, every child is born with a sinful nature. We as parents must teach them to be good, which is against this sinful nature. As noted earlier in this chapter, discipline is an important aspect of shaping and encouraging the child to resist the natural inclination toward evil.

Encouraging children toward what God wants eventually becomes an act of the will—a decision for or against Christ. We must never forget that they (and we) will live somewhere—either heaven or hell—forever. Yet a decision about salvation is not likely to occur before the school years, although there are some remarkable (though rare) examples where people have become Christians in their preschool years. While they are infants and toddlers we must concentrate on helping them to move in the right direction, rather than making a decision they are mentally incapable of. We must pave the way so that salvation will be easier to accept later.

As mentioned in the previous chapter, the home environment is vitally important for babies spiritually. Caring for the child's emotional and physical needs is foundational for spiritual development later in life. While the infant does not understand religious concepts or have religious beliefs, our religious beliefs and concepts strongly influence the way we act toward the infant. The baby can sense the overall home atmosphere and emotionally link it with our religious words and practices.

The attachment to the parents is vital to later faith because attachment produces security. When someone, usually the mother, consistently takes care of a baby's needs and gives emotional support, the child is not only more trusting (as mentioned in the last chapter) but also more able to meet the world confidently. Trust and confidence are basic foundations for faith, as has been noted by a number of researchers (Ratcliff 1992a).

The understanding of God makes an interesting reversal during the toddler and preschool years. At first infants and toddlers see parents as having divine characteristics. When they are regularly available to the child, parents appear to be all-powerful, all-knowing, and everywhere all the time. Eventually, with good spiritual training, the child will transfer these ideas to God. How important it is that we parents set the stage for a positive understanding of God by being loving, caring, but also concerned about obedience and respect during these early years. We are the only picture of God our infants and toddlers can comprehend. If we are gone most of the day, what does this communicate about God? If parents are harsh and critical, never satisfied with the child's behavior, what does this communicate? Keep in mind that this picture of God will be accepted more at an emotional level than at a mental level by young children, a picture that will influence them to some extent throughout life. The relationship with the parents powerfully affects future concepts of God.

What can we do to encourage faith in God? During these years parents can teach the youngster to say a memorized prayer, although he or she is probably thinking more about Daddy than God the Father. One must also be careful about what comes into the toddler's ears and eyes from television and music played in the home. Regular displays of violence and immorality are likely to shape the child's understanding of reality in ways that may negatively influence future spiritual development. On the other hand, a few good music tapes or Christian television programs or videotapes, especially if designed for younger children, can be helpful. They need to be used sparingly; toddlers require plenty of one-to-one interaction with loving parents.

What about church activities at this age? Most of the time in church should be spent in supervised play activities. Good, safe, clean toys are a must. We need well-trained, loving teachers at this level, not just teenage girls who want to skip church. For toddlers, a simple story or two from the Bible may be good, and coloring pictures from the story can be interesting. Churches and parents need to infuse "God words" into the play of toddlers. For example, when a two-year-old puts a teddy bear or doll to bed, we can speak of being thankful to God for night and sleep. The goal is not complete comprehension, but positive associations with the words of our faith.

Toddlers can learn simple songs with lots of clapping and jumping, such as "Jesus Loves Me," and the old spiritual "I Put On My Walking Shoes." As a special treat, the pastor may want to stop by to hold, talk to, and play with the kids.

What should parents do when toddlers refuse to stay in their Sunday school class? The key concern is whether refusal is rebellion or insecurity. Assure the child you will return. You might leave the child crying, then wait just outside the room for a few minutes to see if the crying stops shortly. If engaged in interesting activities by a loving, trustworthy teacher, it should cease within a couple of minutes. But if it doesn't, it may be best to spend a few Sundays with the child in the classroom. This will help the toddler get used to the new environment and minimize the possibility of negative associations with the church. We must never forget that the earliest impressions of church at this age can emotionally influence the child for the rest of life. Spanking a toddler for making noise in church may do irreparable harm—quality nursery care makes a lot more sense.

4

Preschoolers

Emma Beth, now a *toddler*, is very different from her brother Stephen when he was a *preschooler*. When we play lively music, Beth jumps and turns excitedly with her whole body. Stephen, like most preschoolers, learned to do intricate hand motions corresponding to the words of the music. Beth makes broad strokes when coloring, ignoring the lines of the picture; Stephen carefully tried to stay within the lines and succeeded much of the time. Over the next couple of years Beth will need help with dressing, but like Stephen she will learn skills such as zipping and buttoning clothes, tying shoes, and tooth brushing without help. To help preschoolers learn these things, buy clothes that make zipping, buttoning, and other aspects of putting on clothes easier (Wallinga and Skeen 1988, 31). They will still need help deciding what to wear.

Preschoolers do not change clothing sizes as often as they did in toddlerhood because the rate of growth slows down. They don't eat quite as much as they did earlier, although this makes it very important that the food they do eat is nutritious.

Many other things change during the preschool years as well. Stephen outgrew his nap—he would sleep a couple of hours in the afternoon at age three, but only a half hour or so by five. Preschoolers still need plenty of sleep at night—about ten to twelve hours or so. Stephen began showing a clear preference for his right hand by about age four, as do 90 percent of children (if children prefer the left, it is unwise to try to change them). Preschoolers will still wiggle and be bored with church, so junior church or some other alternative to the standard service activity is needed. Children's nervous systems become more fully developed, so they hear and see more details (Wallinga and Skeen 1988, 30–32). Sometimes we have to answer Beth's question a dozen times before she understands, older preschoolers may only need to be told once (if they listen the first time).

During the preschool years, from age three to six, the child takes great strides in becoming more self-sufficient. Youngsters feed themselves and even cut most of their own food. By the early preschool period most children are completely toilet-trained, using the bathroom when they need to, cleaning themselves afterward, and not wetting the bed most nights. They are also less dependent upon parents as their circle of relationships broadens to include more friends and perhaps a preschool teacher.

Mental Development

Reasoning ability grows rapidly between the ages of three and six. During these years the child begins to reason things out concretely, but the knowledge of abstract concepts is still almost nil. Because of their concrete reasoning everything is either right or wrong, there are no shades of gray. Without a good environment, including good education and parenting, many people never outgrow this way of thinking.

To some extent the child still imagines that others see things the way the child sees them. For example, the preschooler may wonder why supper is not ready at the moment the child gets hungry, or suppose that everyone lives exactly the way they do (Fitch and Ratcliff 1991, 157).

The child is also easily misled by the appearances of things. In his classic experiment, Jean Piaget found that most preschoolers thought the amount of water changed when it was poured from one size container to another. One of our students remarked that her preschool son complained he did not get as much milk as the older sister because the level of liquid was higher in the sister's thinner glass! What that student saw was almost an exact copy of Piaget's experiment. Preschoolers often look only at the appearance of things in making conclusions and decisions, something the Bible tells adults to avoid: "Man looks at the outward appearance, but the Lord looks at the heart" (1 Sam. 16:7).

Children at this age learn by example. Not only do they imitate their parents, brothers and sisters, and friends, but they also need a number of examples to learn new ideas. The Bible teaches by example—consider the Bible "hall of fame" in Hebrews 11. Use good examples to teach new ideas at this age (Ratcliff 1988a, 9).

Using the word "why?" signals the beginning of cause and effect reasoning. At two-and-one-half, Emma Beth used this word but really did not understand what it meant. One time her mommy asked her why she was jumping so much. She replied, "jumping, jumping." Mommy replied, "But tell me why," to which Beth replied, "why!" When preschoolers begin asking why, it may be good to encourage them to try to figure out why instead of immediately telling them the answer. Parents weary of all the "whys" at this age, but you may be encouraged to learn that this signals a new advancement in their thinking.

Memory improves for preschoolers, and they can often remember three or four things at once. If you are teaching your youngster a Bible verse, have them learn it three or four words at a time rather than the six or seven that adults can handle. And be sure they can understand what they are reciting. Memory improves when things are repeated, so when your son or daughter wants you to read the same Bible story over and over, do it. It may be old hat for you, but they will remember it much better, perhaps for the rest of their lives. Acting out the story also helps them remember it better (more on this later).

Distance is often confused with time for preschoolers (Piaget 1971). "Long ago in a far away land" could mean last week across town! These things must be kept in mind when preschoolers are told stories or when we ask them to come in "soon"—they simply have little or no understanding of time at this age.

Language

During the preschool years language develops rapidly with the child adding hundreds of words to his or her vocabulary every year. Even though they do not understand a lot of words, they try to make sense of what they hear. For example, a child told his father that in church they sang a song about a bear named Gladly who had crossed eyes. This puzzled the father until he realized his son was talking about the hymn "Gladly the Cross I'd Bear!" Children do their best to make sense out of what we tell them.

Children sometimes may appear to disobey when actually they have not really heard what you asked them to do or not do. They may hear only certain words the adult speaks, not the entire sentence, partly because the preschooler memory can only include about three or four words at a time. Children at this age often guess what people say by looking at the social situation (Shatz 1978). They try to make some meaning out of the few words they do hear, but the meaning they construe may be vastly different from what the parent actually said. How can you be sure they really understand what you say? Try having them repeat back to you the statement you made if what you asked is new or a bit unusual (this may be needed with older children as well).

Should you correct poor grammar? Research (Cazden 1972) shows that it does not result in more correct speech. There is also the danger that you will discourage communication if you make incorrect grammar a big issue; correction can be seen as punishment that can affect the parent/child relationship. Actually, children may use correct grammar and then begin to use poor grammar because they are learning more about language, a temporary reversal that helps them in the long run. For example, the child may say "I saw a horse" and a few weeks later state "I sawed my friend." Actually that is an advancement, because he or she is learning that we add the "ed" when it occurred in the past. When you hear grammatical mistakes, you might repeat the sentence correctly for the child, so they will hear it in the right form, but don't overly emphasize the mistake. Eventually they will pick up the correct grammar if they hear it enough from others.

What else can help your child learn more words and understand them better? Try reading them stories from books that have a lot of pictures. Talk around the dinner table, and include the preschooler in the conversation; never watch television while you eat. When the child watches television, talk about the show during commercials. It also helps language development to explain what is happening when you are watching something take place, and then having the child repeat your words (Coates and Hartup 1969).

Social and Emotional Characteristics

People need people. Those who lack good relationships are not mentally healthy—usually they are lonely, empty, lack purpose, and suffer from emotional pain. Therefore parents need to teach their preschooler social skills by exposing the child to other children, preferably of the same age and sex.

During toddlerhood and up to age three or so the child will play next to other children, but not really play with them. They may talk to one another, but usually each one is talking about a different topic. Playing side by side is called *parallel play.* But later, at age four and five, they begin to play with each other, such as playing house or cops and robbers. They also talk to one another on the same topics. This is called *cooperative play.* This change in play shows that the child is less self-centered and is able to imagine another person's viewpoint to some extent. Think of it: to play house, one must be able to understand not only one's own role (daddy) but also how that relates to other roles (mommy, children, and so on). Cooperative play shows the child is growing in his or her view of the social world. Playing house can also give parents a picture of how the child understands family life and things that take place in life.

Gary Collins (1971, 50) suggests four benefits of play in childhood.

1. It permits discharge of energy.
2. It provides needed stimulation.
3. It helps children develop motor skills.
4. It enables the child to act out and learn to understand adult roles.

Without question, play is not just nonsense: it is an important window to the child's understanding, and a valuable means of learning. Rousseau once said that play is the preschooler's work.

Emotions are also a very important part of the life of preschoolers. Preschoolers are likely to express their emotions more freely than many adults who have learned to suppress them. Preschoolers experience fears, anxiety, jealousy, curiosity, joy, and primitive forms of love.

Preschools, Kid Swapping, and Preparing for School

While we spoke out strongly against day care in the last chapter, some time in a preschool may be helpful for three- to five-year-olds. It is important that the preschool program *not* be high-paced and accelerated because these are likely to produce "burnout" and lack of interest in learning by the time the child is in third or fourth grade (Elkind 1987). Notice the emphasis on *some* time. All day, every day instruction is still inappropriate, as it can contribute to a "herd mentality," excessive conformity that will continue into the school years. There is also danger that certain kinds of preschools can cause psychological damage. Psychiatrists Freedman, Kaplan, and Sadock (1972, 668) state, "inadequate facilities or personnel may be destructive to the proper psychological growth and development of children." Perhaps the government should require all preschools and day-care centers to post that message on their doors, just like the warnings on cigarettes!

On the other hand, two or three mornings away from mother at this age may not only do the child some good but will give mom a little break. If you put your child in a preschool, be sure it has warm, loving, well-trained, multiple mother substitutes. Even at the best preschools, though, you can expect children to pick up more diseases and probably some vulgar words that will have to be corrected.

Some parents prefer to swap child care with a neighbor or friend instead of sending the child to preschool. This may work well a couple of mornings a week, and give the kids added time with other children. I did this with my children and found it worked well.

What can parents do to get kids ready for schooling? Reading simple books to them will help, especially if you pause during the story and ask questions about what is happening (Bruner 1986). This helps prepare them for the question and answer format they will use during the school years.

As noted above, the parent or preschool teacher should not try to teach a lot of academic subjects. Instead children can learn the social skills of cooperation, sharing, and give and take as they play together. The parent or teacher might help them learn a few prereading skills, such as reciting and recognizing letters and numbers, but plan on gradually introducing these over a period of several months. If the child catches on quickly and wants to learn more, you could try teaching the sounds of letters and simple addition using objects. Again, if they begin getting frustrated and tired with this kind of learning, *stop!* They have plenty of time to learn it later. In fact, a number of studies described by Raymond and Dorothy Moore (1979) suggest that children learn academic subjects faster and better if they do not begin school until eight years of age! They suggest parents home school prior to eight, with emphasis upon social relationships and experiencing the world around them rather than formal learning.

Emotional Reactions to Violence

In an experiment at the University of Georgia, researchers (Osborn and Endsley 1971) studied the emotional reactions of young children to TV violence. They showed three brief, violent TV episodes to four- and five-year-old children while measuring how much the children sweat. The children were also shown two nonviolent films. As measured by the sweating, the children responded more emotionally to the violent films and remembered them better one week later. The emotion aroused by the violent films was primarily fear. Violent scenes with human characters aroused more fear than did violent scenes with cartoon characters. The children were able to recall twice as many details about the human violence than anything else they saw. This implies that when something triggers the emotions, it is more likely to be remembered later. The main lesson, perhaps, is that what we feed our children's minds will be there for years to come, especially if it stirs emotions.

Just about everything is on television these days. A great deal of it is simply not appropriate for children. While the media generally maintains that the violent and sexual nature of most of the programs does not affect children's behavior, the success of television advertising says just the opposite. Sales of Reeses "Pieces" skyrocketed just because they were portrayed for a couple of minutes in the movie "E.T." (even without naming them). Clearly what our children see on either the big screen or small screen can potentially affect their behavior. We must carefully monitor and control what we allow them to see and hear.

Personality Development

As we saw in the last chapter, the mother is especially important for personality development in infancy and toddlerhood. While the father needs to be involved in child-rearing from day one, he takes an even more central place in the personality development of children during the preschool years. Christian fathers should spend much time with their sons and daughters. Research indicates that children at this age who lose their fathers (through divorce, death, or too many hours away from home) are affected for many years afterward. For example, Hall, Lamb, and Perlmutter (1986, 417) quote studies showing that preschool boys without fathers are more feminine, avoid competition, and "have difficulty establishing a long-term heterosexual relationship" as an adult. Preschool girls without fathers are more likely to be either extremely shy or become very seductive in adolescence. Emotional problems are commonly the result of father absence (Nicholi 1985). George Rekers (1986), in testimony before the United States Congress, provides evidence that children who lack fathers are also more likely to have intellectual difficulties and adjustment problems. Elsewhere (Rekers 1982) he describes a wide variety of studies that also show how devastating father absence is to children.

It is sad to see how Hollywood and the television networks are attacking fathers today. The typical father, as seen on the TV screen in homes today, is either extremely violent or a powerless wimp. Movies, such as "The Little Mermaid," increasingly tell children that they need not obey their parents (Yoest 1992, 66). How far we have come from the days of the Waltons and the Cleavers!

In any Christian's home, a boy's best friend should be his father, and a girl's best friend her mother. It is especially important for fathers to spend large amounts of time with their preschool boys and mothers with preschool girls because these are the years in which children come to identify with their own sex. They need a parent of their own sex to imitate.

We take identifying with one's own sex for granted. When people fail to accept their given gender, this is considered a mental disorder (Meier, Minirth, and Ratcliff 1992, 136–37 and 154–55) and is often associated with a great deal of emotional pain. One of our jobs as parents is to help our children accept and value their sexual identities. Yet everywhere in our society this is being threatened, not only by the absence of parents but also through the unisex movement. It is sometimes hard to tell a boy from a girl today, but the Bible states that boys should dress like boys and girls like girls (Deut. 22:5). And, although no chores are exclusively masculine or feminine, encourage your boys to help daddy with his chores and your girls to help mommy with hers. It is also good to compliment daughters for looking feminine and boys for looking masculine, although praise should primarily be reserved for the quality of behavior and character, not appearance. Accepting one's gender is also encouraged by preschoolers having friends who are the same sex.

Sometimes preschool children come to think that somehow they will eventually marry the parent of the opposite sex. While Freud's old theory of childhood sexuality exaggerated this idea, many children do have this fantasy. Probably the best response is to matter-of-factly tell the child that this will not happen, but that they are loved by both mommy and daddy. It is probably a good idea to not let preschool children sleep with the opposite sex parent (a practice more common than might be thought) and also that parents insist on more privacy in dressing, using the restroom, and bathing.

What is most harmful is when boys whose mothers are either no longer married or not close to their husbands, are unconsciously made little husbands for their mothers. This also sometimes occurs between fathers and daughters. Even if there is no sexual aspect of such a relationship, it is asking children to take on a role that is simply inappropriate. They often suffer emotionally for the rest of their lives. Parents should also not belittle or put down one gender or the other.

Parents are very important to children at this age. Some have said that they think the quality of time spent with their kids is more important than quantity. All we can say to that is "nonsense." A large quantity of time is essential, and if you can improve the quality during that large quantity of time, well so much the better. Some have suggested that when both parents work, they are more likely to get down on the floor and play with the child than is the stay-at-home mother. Several research studies indicate this is far from the truth (Yoest 1992, 21). Parents cannot possibly have energy and time for kids when they arrive home tired and worn out from a full day of work to be greeted by all the household chores yet to do. Interestingly, research indicates that even working fathers spend more time with their children when mom stays at home (Nock and Kingston 1988). What is most important is that at least one parent be available when children need them, not just in the evening or on a weekend, even if most of the time is not spent on the floor playing with them.

Defense Mechanisms

Like adults, children see the world through a microscope. The human mind is highly selective, relying on specific impressions of what is factual and real, rather than what is actually the truth. Decisions are based on past experiences, conscious perceptions, prejudices, conscious and unconscious drives, emotions, social pressures, mental capacity to interpret reality, and many other factors. No one can see things the way they really are 100 percent of the time, although we are promised in Scripture that one day we will know "even as I am fully known" (1 Cor. 13:12).

One way people disguise the truth from others (and themselves) is through defense mechanisms. While these first begin in childhood, they continue throughout life. People with healthy personalities keep defense mechanisms to a minimum, but nearly everyone uses them at least occasionally. Children who have experienced the unpleasant feelings of anxiety or depression will look for ways to prevent those unpleasant feelings from recurring, thus they use defense mechanisms.

The most basic defense mechanism is *repression*. This involves the banishment of unpleasant thoughts from the conscious mind. For example, a preschooler (or any age child) may resent the birth of a new baby brother by saying, "I wish he was never born" or even "Why doesn't he die?" Since these thoughts are shocking to the parents, they may respond "Oh, you don't really think that" or "What a terrible thing to say!" Thus, to please the parents, a child may banish those very real feelings from the conscious mind, telling himself that he does not have those thoughts, repressing those ideas. It would be healthier for parents to try to find out why the child feels that way. They may even want to affirm the child by saying, "Yes, it is hard to not be the center of attention any longer." The resentment may, in fact, be an indication that one of the parents needs to spend more time with the child, as well as encourage him or her to see the positive aspects of the new brother.

Another defense mechanism that makes an early appearance is *regression*. When children encounter something that makes them insecure, such as the parents arguing loudly, they may begin acting as they did at an earlier stage of development when they felt more secure. They may begin to wet the bed or suck the thumb long after they quit doing those things. These forms of regression often occur with older children as well, especially when a new baby is born.

Denial surfaces quite early with children as well, a defense mechanism that is common at all ages. The child (or adult) simply refuses to admit the fact that something disturbs them, even though it clearly does. For example, children may refuse to admit they are angry, in spite of the obvious fact that they are.

One other defense mechanism that surfaces in early childhood is *projection*, which is attributing one's own impulses or wishes to someone else. Thus the youngster who feels hostile toward his older brother, but does not want the uncomfortable feelings that accompany hostile wishes, will convince himself that it is really his brother who is angry at him. The same thing could happen with the parent—the child may be upset with the parent, but think the parent is angry instead. Of course it can also go the other way—parents may imagine problems in their children that are really their own hidden desires, such as the father of a teenage girl that mistakenly thinks she is sexually active. The parent may have unconsciously wished he was having an affair. Christ referred to this defense mechanism when he said: "Do not judge, or you too will be judged. . . . Why do you look at the speck of sawdust in your brother's eyes and pay no attention to the plank in your own eye?" (Matt. 7:1, 3).

Discipline

In the last chapter we emphasized the value of spanking, which should also be used during the preschool years. However, at any age it can be overused until it no longer works very well. This kind of punishment is far more effective if used only occasionally for clear-cut defiance. In addition, explanation of what was done wrong and why it was wrong should be provided. Give the child an opportunity to talk about the situation to correct possible misunderstandings (but don't let the child talk you out of deserved punishment!). Afterward, let the child cry and give affection if the child wants it.

Effective parents use a variety of discipline methods, not just one. Keep in mind that good discipline is not just to get rid of bad behavior, but also to instill good, alternative behavior. Thus praise, attention, and occasional rewards for positive, desirable actions are just as important as punishment for the bad.

One possible discipline technique is ignoring improper behavior. Sometimes attention of any kind makes an undesired action more likely to happen. We have seen some neglected children misbehave simply because it was the only way they would get attention. Even a spanking is better than neglect, they feel. Thus attention can be a powerful reward. In some cases, simply refusing to pay attention to aggravating behavior makes it less likely to happen in the future. This is not always effective, but it comes in handy at times.

Isolation is an old standby for parents. Sitting on a stool for a few minutes can seem like an eternity to an active preschooler. Standing in the corner, going to the bedroom, and other forms of isolation can be effective ways to help the child obey. Be careful that the isolation is not rewarding, though, or it will not work. For example, if the child acts rudely and is sent to her room where she can play video games, she really has not been punished. Also be careful not to overdo the isolation—a good rule of thumb is that isolation should last the number of minutes equal to the child's age in years. Thus a four-year-old should not be isolated for more than four minutes at a time. Finally, don't place the child in a frightening situation, such as a dark closet. Discipline should be effective but not traumatic.

Deprivation is another discipline technique to consider. Taking away favorite toys for a few days, going without dessert after supper, not letting the child go outside for awhile, or not allowing the child to participate in a favorite activity may all be effective methods of discipline. It is a good idea to link deprivation with the misdeed whenever possible, such as taking away dessert because food was purposefully spilled on the floor, hiding a favorite doll because it was not put away, or not playing ball with the child when he refuses to share the ball with others.

Effective parents use a variety of discipline methods, and do not get stuck with only one. Variety makes each method more likely to work. Some methods are more effective for some children than others, but to use only one is to ask for problems. And, finally, good parents are careful to include a lot of positive, affirming, and encouraging comments and actions in their day to day activities with their children. Punishment is most effective when it comes from warm, loving parents (Hall, Lamb, and Perlmutter 1986, 407).

What does not do much good is prolonged reasoning about misconduct, in fact this is a futile waste of time. They cannot begin to think abstractly until they are into the school years. If we try to reason about the moral concept they have disobeyed, their minds are at least a mile away. A quick spanking or other form of discipline, severe enough to bring repentance, is much more effective in dealing with children this age.

Typical Problems

Fears and Nightmares

Like toddlers, preschoolers also have a number of fears, including fears of animals, monsters, and even storybook characters ("the big bad wolf"). They have trouble separating fact and fantasy and may need to be reassured over and over by their parents of safety.

Nightmares and night terrors are quite common in preschoolers. Because there are many things that a three- to six-year-old does not yet understand, a larger portion of sleep time is spent dreaming and thus sleep disturbance is more likely. Most children have these problems at one time or another. Night terrors involve thrashing around in bed and crying out, but unlike nightmares, the children do not wake themselves up. In fact, you may have a hard time waking them up during a night terror even if you shake them. Most children have them for only a short period of time; they go away as the conflicts causing them are resolved. Medication can be given to eliminate night terrors during this period of time, but usually this is not necessary. We recommend that you keep a nightlight in your preschooler's room so he or she can see that there aren't any animals or bogeymen. If your child comes to your bed at night after a nightmare, take the youngster back to his or her own bed and calmly talk to the child for a few minutes. Sleep walking is also common in young children, and is nothing to worry about if they stay in the house! Medications can stop this also.

Temper Tantrums

Between three and four years of age (if not before) children learn to throw temper tantrums. I recall the day that this first happened with my oldest son, then about three years old. A neighbor girl, about the same age, had visited him for most of the afternoon. When her mommy told her it was time to come home, she fell to the floor kicking, crying, and demanding to stay. The embarrassed mother gave in to the little one's demand. You could almost see the wheels turning inside my son's head. He must have thought, "looks like a neat way to get what you want." Sure enough, the next day he gave it a try. The tactic did not work nearly so well for him; temper tantrums did not pay off for him; he didn't get what he wanted and he got something else he certainly did not want!

Temper tantrums continue only if they pay off in some way. They can become a way of life, with even parents of teenagers giving in to avoid a "scene." We are all motivated by rewards—would you continue your job without a paycheck?—and the same is true for preschoolers. The reward for tantrums is getting their way.

If you do not want temper tantrums for the rest of the child's life, you need to take appropriate action as soon as possible after each tantrum. For some children, simply refusing to give in is sufficient; ignoring is enough. Others will throw an even bigger temper tantrum when you ignore their out-of-control behavior. In that case you might grab them firmly by the shoulders and tell them to stop it, or even spank them if needed. Eliminating the reward is often sufficient, because the tantrums no longer serve a useful function.

Sexuality

Children often ask questions about sex-related things at this age, and—as we saw in toddlerhood—the healthy thing to do is answer them truthfully and matter-of-factly without showing embarrassment. You should not go on and tell them things they did not ask for, but answer their questions accurately and specifically. Teach them that some things are talked about privately and done privately. For example, we should not allow our children at this age to run around in the yard without any clothes on. Yet, if we find them in that situation, we should not become agitated and angry; simply tell them to put their clothes on again. If we find our child examining the genitals in bed at night when we happen to walk in on them, the best thing to do is ignore it or politely ask the youngster to leave the pajamas on.

Boys and girls often want to explore the differences between their bodies at this age. Most of us had the same tremendous curiosity about the physical differences of the opposite sex in the preschool years, though many of us have long repressed those memories. What is most crucial is that curiosity, not sexual arousal, is behind the exploring behavior. If you discover your child has been examining another's genitals, encourage them to talk about it. Affirm their own gender, as well as the interest in the opposite sex, but firmly let them know that they should not continue this private exploration with the friend. Some parents have found that bathing two preschoolers of the opposite sex together, with parent supervision, helps satisfy curiosity in a healthy manner. Of course, this should only be done with the permission and preferably the presence of the other child's parents. Sometimes a better alternative is to babysit an infant of the opposite sex and allow the preschooler to watch when changing the diaper.

Bedwetting and Soiling

Even though many children are successfully toilet trained before the preschool years, bedwetting is still a very common problem during the preschool years. About 88 percent quit wetting their beds by the time they are four-and-one-half years of age, but about 8 to 10 percent still wet their beds from time to time when they reach six years of age, about 1 to 2 percent even after high school graduation (Freedman and Kaplan 1967, 1380). The best thing to do when this happens is have the child clean up his or her own bed, as much as is possible, but do not shame the child. You might also consider buying one of the "bell and pad" sets available from some sales catalogs, which rings a bell when the child wets the bed. The noise helps the child become aware of the release of urine from a full bladder. After using it for awhile, most children learn to wake themselves up when the bladder is full. Other guidelines for toilet training are found in the previous chapter of this book.

Soiling the bed, like bedwetting, can be expected in the preschool years. We would encourage you to remember that the age at which children are biologically ready for toilet training varies from one-and-one-half to four years of age. Thus soiling is not considered abnormal unless the child is past four years old. If your child is over four and still soiling from time to time, it would be best to get treatment from a child psychiatrist, or a pediatric specialist if the problem is due to physical problems.

Handicaps

Handicapped children are usually affected psychologically by the specific handicaps they have (Bentovim 1972, 634). Handicapped children frequently become very dependent, passive, and somewhat withdrawn. Sometimes handicapped children become scapegoats who the family teases and rejects.

Children who are physically handicapped often develop problems in their everyday behavior. For example, they may become frustrated and express that frustration in angry words or actions, blame others, withdraw by fantasizing a lot of the time, or become immature in their actions. In addition, they may become timid and self-conscious and react in more extreme ways than average children (Kirk 1972).

Another handicap sometimes found with preschoolers is some kind of vision problem. If your child rubs the eyes a great deal all day long, or you find him or her tilting the head or covering one eye quite a bit, this may indicate a sight problem. A lot of blinking, squinting, or holding books close to the eyes may also show eye problems. Crossed eyes, problems with eyelids, itching, burning, watery, or red eyes also may spell problems in this area, as can complaints about double vision, blurring, dizziness, or headaches when working on something.

Preschoolers can also have hearing loss. If they complain of earaches, ringing in the ear, dizziness, sudden hearing loss, or if they hear better when they can see you, check with a doctor. Often children that do not hear well do not pay attention as well as other children, and ask adults to repeat things a lot. Turning the head a great deal, leaning forward to hear better, interrupting conversations, poor speech or speech that is too loud or soft, and withdrawing when speech is required may possibly show that there are problems in this area. These kids may also have a hard time telling where a sound is coming from, and sometimes confuse numbers that have similar sounds such as 15 and 16, or 50 and 60. Check with a doctor if you think there may be problems in this area.

Too often handicapped children find that parents and others let them have their own way because they feel sorry for them, breeding selfishness and self-centeredness. If you have a handicapped child, don't deny the handicap, but encourage independence. And don't pity the child—love the youngster and trust the child's ability to either successfully cope with the handicap or overcome it, as well as to become a responsible individual.

Child Abuse

The Bible is clearly against child abuse and neglect. Consider the following passage: "And whoever welcomes a little child like this in my name welcomes me. But if anyone causes one of these little ones who believe in me to sin, it would be better for him to have a large millstone hung around his neck and to be drowned in the depths of the sea" (Matt. 18:5–6).

Although punishment is clearly equated with good parenting in the Bible, abuse is not. It is interesting to study some of the customs of the Canaanites and other surrounding cultures in Old Testament times. Horrible abuse, even killing of children was apparently fairly common. The accounts of sacrifices to the false gods Molech and Baal were often sacrifices of young children (Jer. 19:4–5; 32:35). Against this historical background, the Old Testament statements about discipline are very mild and child-affirming! Terrible abuse characterized the Romans, which again makes the New Testament concern for children a tremendous contrast (Clapp 1984).

Single Parenting

Another very serious problem in the United States is single-parent families. More than one in four American children are now in homes with only one parent, and in the black community the rate is an astounding 68 percent. These high rates for blacks and whites alike are not only because of the high divorce rate, but also the rapidly escalating number of births to unmarried women (Yoest 1992, 23).

The result is a disaster for children. A number of studies have found that children reared in single-parent homes are more likely to be delinquent, have sleep disturbances, get poorer grades in school, use drugs and alcohol, and grow up to have broken marriages (Yoest 1992, 24–25; Whitehead 1993). No matter what the age of the child is at the time of the divorce, it is traumatic.

Judith Wallerstein and Joan Kelly (1980), in their studies of long-term effects of divorce, found that nearly all the children continued to have some difficulty even ten years after their parents were divorced. About one third were seriously disturbed, another third were coping but not fully recovered, and even the healthiest third still experienced loneliness and general unhappiness because of the divorce. These now grown children were likely to have a great deal of anxiety and guilt, as well as a tendency to rush into impulsive relationships. In general, divorce is harder on the children than on either of the adults.

There are so many Christian fathers and mothers who are failing in their responsibilities before God that it makes us grieve. We cannot repeat enough the fact that the father and mother's first responsibility from God is the family. All else comes in a distant second. Paul said that if a Christian does not provide for the needs of his own household, he is "worse than an unbeliever" (1 Tim. 5:8).

Nervous Habits

Don't worry about moderate nail-biting. A good number of college students still bite their nails! Nervous tics, however, such as regular squinting of the eyes, regular jerking of some part of the body, and constant clearing of the throat, may be signs of emotional conflicts requiring counseling. Tics usually go away as the conflicts are resolved. There are also medications that will eliminate many tics within just a few hours, but unless the person deals with the underlying problems the tics will return when the medicine is discontinued.

Stuttering in preschool children is considered normal and should just be ignored. Often the more attention you pay to it, the worse it becomes, because attention may either reward it or make the child more self-conscious. Stuttering nearly always goes away by age six. The reason it occurs so often is that during the preschool years the child's knowledge and vocabulary are increasing much more rapidly than the physical ability to get the words and thoughts expressed. If stuttering continues after age six, consult a speech therapist. Sometimes a psychiatrist can help by prescribing medicines. Even lifelong stuttering in an adult can be eliminated 60 percent of the time within two days after taking a low dosage of Haldol.

Obesity

Our society is obsessed with weight. Just recently a news release stated that nearly all of the major models could be considered borderline anorexics (a mental disease that produces extreme weight loss through self-starvation). The mannequins in most department stores are also extremely thin.

This obsession with thinness has filtered down to our children. A recent television special interviewed a number of nine- and ten-year-old girls who repeatedly commented that they had to be thin to be beautiful, and one skinny youngster openly wept about how fat she thought she looked. No wonder we have an epidemic of anorexia today!

Yet we must also be realistic with our children. While we might want our society to change its views, our children must still live in the real world. As a result, we advise strongly that you avoid obesity in your child at any cost. Being overweight will greatly hamper self-worth and limit respect received from peers. Preschool and elementary-age children are very tactless and will broadcast any defect they see in others. It's not right, but that's the way it is, so let's deal with the problem realistically. But if the child is of average size, don't encourage weight loss. It might help to comment on how the thinness of some people on television is not healthy. It can also help to avoid talking a lot about your own weight! Encourage your children to look on the inner person, rather than outward appearance, as noted earlier.

Depression and Excessive Stress

These two problems are not uncommon among preschoolers. Childhood depression is usually manifested by social withdrawal, continual sadness, and either a marked increase or decrease in activity (Meier, Minirth, and Ratcliff 1992, 154). Depression frequently follows the loss of a loved possession or person (such as in divorce, death, or transfer of the father overseas). Weekly counseling sessions, and low doses of antidepressants, often meet with success.

Everyone has stress, and—as noted earlier—some degree of stress helps psychological development. Preschoolers have many adjustments to make as they reach toward the independence of being school-age. Simple events like going to Sunday school, to the doctor or dentist, moving into a new home, having a new baby brother or sister, can all be very stressful for a preschooler. As a matter of fact, going to the dentist is usually quite stressful for us! The best way we, as parents, can reduce these stresses for our children is to prepare them for these events by talking about them ahead of time in words that children will understand (Collins 1971, 56). Always be truthful. It can even be distressing for children to go to sleep at night, only to wake up to find a strange babysitter there and their parents gone. We always tell our children when we are going out, even if they will be asleep before the babysitter comes, so they won't be surprised.

Spiritual Development

We must bear in mind that the child's reasoning ability, described near the beginning of this chapter, has a powerful effect upon spiritual understanding as well. For example, stories about Jesus and some of the little children in the Bible have a great deal of meaning to children at this age. In contrast, teaching them about abstract concepts like parable interpretation or "agape" love will only make them wish you would hurry up and get done so they can get back to their toys. One researcher, for example, told children the story about Moses and the burning bush. He then asked them what the "holy ground" was that Moses stood on. Some thought it meant there were holes that he could fall into, or that the ground was muddy, and one even thought it meant the ground was soft (Goldman 1964—also see Ratcliff 1987). The more appropriate the spiritual training the child has during these three years, the more he will understand and rely upon his Christian faith when he is older and has meaningfully accepted Jesus Christ as his Savior.

Can a preschooler be saved? We believe some children can understand enough during the latter part of their first six years to know that they are frequently sinful, that they want God to forgive them, and that they want to live forever in heaven. They can put their simple faith in Christ, who taught that unless we as adults have faith like a little child, we will not inherit the kingdom (Luke 18:17). Paul Meier and I both understood enough to put our faith in Christ at ages six and five respectively. We have also personally led to Christ four-, five-, and six-year-olds whom we felt to be genuinely ready for salvation.

As we help our three- to six-year-olds develop spiritually, we must keep in mind that the main sources of their learning, whether at church or at home, are their total life experiences rather than just our words. Gary Collins (1972, 53) states, "A 'loving heavenly father' is foolishness if the child's earthly father is harsh and unkind. . . . Even the child's views of God, Heaven, angels, and Hell are in terms of pictures he has seen."

Therefore, to help children understand Bible stories, and other Christian stories we might tell them, they need to get personally involved. Acting out stories especially helps in understanding them (Ratcliff 1988b, 264–65). As you tell the story, you can pause occasionally and act out the parts with them. If several children are available to play various parts, so much the better. After you finish, you can tell it again and the children can exchange parts. Research indicates that an adult taking part in the acting is important (Ratcliff 1985c), as is the pausing *during* the story to act out what is happening (Villarreal 1982). Acting out parts can also help the child understand church services and family religious rituals.

What are some things from the Bible that preschoolers can learn? My wife Brenda and I have taught four- and five-year-olds simplified versions of the Ten Commandments in a half-day preschool and also in a Sunday school. Nearly every child could remember all ten commandments afterward when they were taught using acting by the kids, stories, coloring pictures, and lots of child-centered applications.

How do children picture God at this age? Often preschoolers and school-age children envision him as a magician in the sky whose purpose is to grant their thoughtless and selfish wishes (Vianello, Tamminen, and Ratcliff 1992). We have known some adults who still pray that way. They try to play God and use God's magic to accomplish *their* will, instead of asking God to show them *his* will in the matter. As we pray with our children, we should show them by our example that prayer is a means of changing our will to make it coincide with the will of God.

During this stage of development, children pick up their notions of what is right or wrong by what they see us doing, not from what we say is right or wrong (Massey 1988, 96–97). For example, we know on the basis of Scripture that there is nothing sinful about feeling the emotion of anger, and we encourage our children to let us know when they feel angry (see Eph. 4:26). If they throw something or hit others due to anger, they get spanked; but if they tell us they are angry toward us or someone else, we thank them for telling us and we talk about it for awhile. Somehow, though, kids sometimes get the idea that anger is wrong. One day the oldest son of Paul Meier watched a television show where a good man became angry over a stolen watermelon. "An hour or two later he came and said, 'Daddy, that man was bad!' I did not know what he was talking about, so I asked him. He told me that the man in the watermelon story was a bad man. 'No he wasn't,' I said, 'he was a good man! What makes you think he was a bad man?' To my dismay he replied, 'He was a bad man because he got angry.' So I explained to him that it's all right to feel angry. It all depends on what we do with that anger."

Holidays

Another thing that can hurt our children's spiritual development is lying to them. This is a terrible thing to do, and yet lying to children is an American tradition, and even Christian families do it. For example, if a child loses a tooth, what do we ask him to do? We tell him that if he will put it under his pillow, a tooth fairy will sneak in at night and put money there. Some Christians tell their preschoolers about the Easter bunny bringing eggs as if it were really true. And when Christmas comes around, the American tradition is to go to all ends to convince our three- to six-year-olds that there is a man called Santa Claus who is omnipresent ("he sees you when you're sleeping"), all-knowing ("he knows when you're awake," "he knows if you've been bad or good"), and all-powerful (he can carry tons of toys all around the world in a matter of hours, flying up and down chimneys). As a result of being taught he has these God-like qualities, Santa Claus becomes an idol that replaces Jesus Christ, whose birthday we are supposedly celebrating (Collins 1972, 55–56). Later, when the child finds out that his Christian parents have been lying about something that has become a major part of their religious beliefs, is it any wonder they have doubts about the things they have been taught about Christianity by the time they are adolescents? Is this a laughing matter? We don't think so.

This does not mean we have to take all the fun out of Christmas. We can play the game of Santa Claus if we make it clear to our children it is only a game. When we go to the department store during the Christmas season, we can say "There's another man dressed up in a funny red suit and beard. Do you want to sit on his lap and get some candy?" If a child asks, "Is there really a Santa Claus, Daddy?" we respond, "No, Santa Claus is just a funny game we play." Our children have just as much fun as other children, but they do not get trapped into praying to him every night and they also know their parents tell the truth about everything.

There are many good ways to celebrate Christmas. There are also a lot of wrong ways to celebrate the birth of Christ. When his children were quite young, Paul Meier would tell them a true story about the birth of Christ while showing them a little manger scene. "Everyone would pray for a minute or two, thanking God for sending Jesus to die on the cross for all the bad things that all of us (daddy included) had done. Then the family would drive around and look at the Christmas lights in town. At home a fire would be lit in the fireplace, everyone ate pistachio ice cream and drank some egg nog, and then we all went to sleep. The next morning, Christmas day, we let the children open a few simple presents that had been sitting under the Christmas tree for days, presents they knew were from mommy and daddy and not from Santa Claus. I told them people give presents to remind others that the wise men brought presents to Jesus, and that Jesus is God's present to us. For preschoolers, that is as deep as I went. When the children got older, I told them other things, such as the fact that Martin Luther was the first man to put an evergreen tree in his home at Christmas, because it was shaped like an arrow pointing up to God in heaven." I like to use an advent wreath with candles to explain Christmas, helping to build anticipation for the birth of Christ over the four weeks before Christmas day.

Some Christians do not give any presents at Christmas because of the materialism involved, and we must admit we don't blame them a bit! They have their fun in other ways, and explain to their children why they don't buy presents for that particular day. We think that's a good idea, but we are satisfied with giving each other some simple gifts—many of them things we need anyway. Some people prefer to give gifts on Christmas eve, or some other day, so children will even more clearly separate Christmas from Santa Claus (as well as allow the children to play with gifts while parents sleep in!).

As with Christmas, we tell our preschool children the Easter story very simply over and over again—how Jesus died and came back to life again, because he is God, and he is still alive and helps us every day. But they can also take part in the local Easter egg hunt and we might even color a few eggs ourselves. We give them buckets or baskets with candy and plastic grass in them.

Another thing we can do to be truthful to our children is to be sure to let them know when we are telling them a fairy tale and when we are telling them a true story. It's very difficult for a young child to separate the two. We believe some of the traditional fairy tales people tell young children can be harmful. All the stories of violence and witches and people cutting off other people's heads can create tremendous fears in three- to six-year-olds who believe mean giants may be hiding in their closets at night. I remember thinking this even as a third grader, and it kept me awake some nights! Television violence, even on children's programs, can also create nightmares and fears.

We should even be selective about what Bible stories we tell our children at each stage of their development. We eventually want them to know all the Bible stories when they are ready to comprehend their significance. Naturally, we don't read them the Song of Solomon, but we might when they are teenagers. The bloody story of Jael (Judg. 4) is obviously inappropriate for little ones (it's even a bit rough for us adults!). As mentioned earlier in this chapter, metaphorical and abstract sections of the Bible cannot be understood by children of this age, and probably not fully comprehended until after ten or eleven. For example, the little song "I will make you fishers of men" actually requires a level of understanding most kids do not have until they are nearly teenagers. Perhaps we spoil the potential appreciation of that vivid, powerful, and beautiful phrase because teens associate it with earlier childish actions.

Finally, we should mention the importance of family devotions with preschoolers. This might include a simple Bible story, brief prayer, and perhaps a time of discussion. The discussion could include talking about the story, the events of the day, or both. Keep it short, pleasant, and simple. Of course, family devotions do not take the place of setting a good example for the child all day long, or of helping the child see how Christianity relates to his or her everyday actions, but family devotions are the capstone to a lived faith. We need a living faith that makes a difference in everything we do, and this can only be taught to a preschooler in the midst of everyday living.

5

The School Years

Stephen, my middle child, is eight years old, well into middle childhood, or "the school years" as it is sometimes called. Between six and twelve his rate of growth will slow even more than during the preschool years. Even so, he can be expected to grow a foot (from four to five feet tall) and double in weight (from 45 to 90 pounds on average). The gain in weight is more muscle than fat, so he will be stronger and more coordinated. His writing is already much improved because the small muscles in his hands are more developed, as well as the nerves throughout his body.

While kids are stronger, their bones are fragile and they actually lose some of the flexibility they had earlier. Children have a lot of injuries and accidents during these years; in fact, injuries are the most likely cause of death at this age. Bones can be twisted and deformed for a lifetime by an overemphasis on sports (especially those that involve throwing). Good warmup exercises can help children avoid such injuries, however. High quality physical education programs at the elementary school level can be healthy for children, as long as there is not too much pressure and the kids are not allowed to tease those who don't do as well.

The biggest change during this age, as suggested by the title of this chapter, is entering elementary school. As noted in the last chapter, it is best for children to spend most of their time outside a classroom until first grade, even though they might attend a preschool a couple mornings a week at age four and a half-day kindergarten at five. With this kind of preparation, and a healthy amount of independence from the mother, all-day schooling in first grade will be more fulfilling than fearful for the child. Some elementary school children must ride the bus to school or have their parents drive them. An extra hour or more in a hot or cold bus should be avoided if at all possible, at least during the early grades.

At this age parents need to make a rather important choice: where to school your child. There are at least three alternatives: public school, a Christian school, or home schooling. There are strong and weak points for each of these that need to be considered.

Perhaps the biggest advantage to public school is that you do not have to spend as much money (although notebooks, pencils, other supplies, and driving them to and from school will cost something). If you send your child to a public school, chances are they will come into contact with many different kinds of children. As a result they will be more likely to understand the natural differences between people. They may also have an opportunity to win others to the Lord, and they may even have an influence upon unsaved teachers. Perhaps you will even be fortunate enough to find a Christian teacher for your child. But plan on correcting poor habits that children easily pick up from unsaved peers, such as cursing, cheating, and so on. Kids will also tend to separate their education from God's truth and the Bible. After a number of years in public education, these are usually thoroughly divorced from one another, even though in reality "all truth is God's truth." Some teachers, even at the elementary level, can influence children away from Christian faith by teaching that one moral view is as good as another (that there is no ultimate truth in life), and other secular ideas.

The desire for combining Christianity with learning makes the Christian school attractive. Children are more likely to have godly teachers and friends in a Christian school, and perhaps they will develop fewer bad habits. Effective discipline is more likely in a Christian school, and they may learn good character traits as well as reading and writing. On the other hand, not all "Christian" schools are fully Christian—some of them teach the secular subjects just like the public schools, even using the same books! Some Christian schools have unqualified teachers because the salaries are so low, and sometimes they admit problem students who can harm your children as much as the public schools. A few Christian schools are overly harsh and rigid, while others are far too permissive. Another obvious drawback is the high cost of tuition.

A third option is home schooling. This approach allows the parents to influence their children more than public and Christian schools, and parents can be more certain that the children get a thoroughly complete and Christian education. There are good teacher's manuals that can help parents teach well, even if they have little or no college education. There are also videotapes and correspondence courses that can help the parent. Research indicates that home schooled kids are more likely to be leaders and do better once they enter school (Moore 1985). The negative side is that some home schooled children may not get enough time with other children, so they might lack some social skills such as cooperation and sharing. Home schooling takes a considerable amount of time from at least one parent. It can also be costly, requiring several hundred dollars a year for materials. Some states have considerable restrictions on home schooling. Finally, some parents simply are not emotionally or mentally up to the task.

Which of these is best? It depends upon the child, the parents, and the quality of schools available in your area. Sometimes a particular child can withstand temptations and influences of ungodly teachers, and you can supplement the secular teaching with Christian values after school. If so, a public school might be best (a good public school may do less harm than a poor Christian school). If a good Christian school is within driving distance, and you can afford it, that might be best. If you have some ability at teaching and would like to be at home with the children all day, home schooling is a good choice. Of course, one of these might work better at some ages than others—for example, you might home school for first and second grades, then send your child to a Christian school. Take special pains to check out your child's first grade teacher. She needs to be a loving, understanding teacher, but also know how to control the class and provide good discipline. Christian or non-Christian, the first teachers will affect the way children look at the education process for the rest of their lives. It's also important for parents and teachers to work together so children will not get two different messages about what is right and wrong.

Mental Development

Mental development is one of the things to consider when making decisions about where to school your child. During the school years, certain areas of the brain mature that allow children to begin doing formal school work. This includes reading, arithmetic, writing, and other important skills. These skills are unlikely to be learned until the brain matures, regardless of how they are taught. For many children, these abilities take longer to develop because the brain is a bit behind schedule; they are just as smart as the others, but they will not do all the same things at the same time. Many boys and some girls have this problem, often indicated by not reading well (or not at all), and they might write some of their letters backward, until the nerves in their brain become mature. These kids are sometimes called "late bloomers," their abilities "bloom" a year or two later than other kids.

My son Stephen is a smart boy, but he did not learn to read at age six. He just could not seem to get the hang of putting letters together with sounds, and my wife and I saw it was hurting his self-concept to push him in this area. He was unable to sit still and concentrate for very long. If he had gone to a standard classroom, I fear that he might have been mislabeled "hyperactive," treated differently by the teacher, and teased by other children. He might have been branded "slow" for the rest of his life.

We decided to home school him for awhile. We encouraged him to look at picture books, and now and then we worked on prereading skills such as learning the sounds of letters, but we didn't push him. We also talked to him about right and wrong, helped him explore some of his own interests, and encouraged him to learn good social skills, such as cooperating and taking turns with his brother and sister, as well as other children. Much of the time he ran and played outside, eventually building himself a tree house. By the end of first grade he had gained some ability at reading, but he was extremely slow. It was almost painful for him to read to us because each word, even each part of a word, took such a long time for him.

About halfway through second grade, when he was about seven-and-one-half or eight, his reading suddenly came alive. Almost overnight he began reading faster and with fewer mistakes. Within a few weeks he was reading all day long, book after book, at about two years above his grade level. He is now in a fine Christian school, and keeps up with the school's advanced level of learning (about two years ahead of the public schools). How glad we are that we did not push him too hard or force him to attend school when most other children begin!

Dr. Raymond Moore (1985), a professional educator and researcher, recommends that children generally not enter school until age eight or later. This is because many children have a difficult time learning in a standard classroom at six or seven years of age. Between 10 and 40 percent of children are, like Stephen, not physically ready for reading and other skills until after first grade (Golden 1981, 181). What a tragedy to damage the self-concepts of these children, perhaps for a lifetime, because of poor decisions about school. Golden also believes that long-term learning problems, such as dyslexia (a reading disorder), can sometimes be the result of pushing "late bloomers" before they are ready. This also shows what a serious mistake it is to push children to learn academics at the preschool level—no wonder they are tired and frustrated with learning long before they are even teenagers (Elkind 1987). It is amazing that more people do not realize that the more we push earlier and earlier education, the more the national test scores go downward!

Social and Emotional Development

During the elementary school years the child develops a real sense of belonging. Group participation, especially with other Christian children, should be encouraged. They can develop a sense of responsibility if they share chores with older brothers and sisters. A sense of belonging and the development of responsibility may help produce leadership abilities in the child. One must learn to obey before one can lead effectively.

The peer group, made up of same-age friends and classmates, is increasingly important at this age. If the child was placed in an all-day preschool, by the elementary school years he or she may have developed a "herd mentality" in which the child simply agrees with peers without thinking. The self-concept is also powerfully affected by peers at this age—kids see themselves through the eyes of friends and classmates as well as parents, teachers, and other adults.

Yet it is quite common for elementary school children to be vicious with one another. Calling one another names and exaggerating the slightest defects are very common. Each child's name is somehow twisted into some awful distortion. Sometimes several children will turn on a classmate with terrible teasing and ridicule. Parents and teachers have a responsibility to teach their children to avoid this practice, encouraging them to see how hurtful it can be. Adults should also intervene when they see this occurring on the playground or at home—the teasing and put-downs are often remembered for many years afterward, scarring the self-concept permanently.

When younger elementary-age children play games such as football, basketball, or baseball, they often have poor organization, heated disputes over rules, lopsided scores, and accusations of cheating. They like to win but must also learn teamwork—the important ability to work together for a common cause with fellow human beings. They also like to play marbles and exchange comic books. We encourage you to buy your children some Christian comic books at this age, as this may give them an opportunity to witness to other children about Christ. They are not too young to do this. But you should probably avoid other kinds of comic books. Many of them are unhealthy morally and sexually. Even some of the comic book characters we all grew up with are no longer wholesome. This holds true for cartoons on television as well. Some Christians have made it a policy to only let their children see Christian cartoons, such as Gerbert, Flying House, and Superbook. Unless you plan to watch the cartoons to screen them carefully (and explain to your kids why certain parts are bad), we suggest you stay with the

Christian programs. This is also true for videos and television programs in general.

David Elkind (1981) emphasizes how people today tend to encourage children to grow up too soon. Childhood is not the time for children to do the things expected of teens and adults like dating and being fashion conscious. Television programs teach children all about adult concerns long before they are ready for them. Sometimes the youngsters portrayed use adult humor and attempt to act like adults. Let kids be kids!

Personality Development

During the elementary school years the child identifies with the parent of the same sex, if that parent is available to the child. Kids also identify with other people of the same gender. Hero worship is to be expected at this age, so it is important to provide the child with appropriate heroes. Parents can do this by praising certain individuals worthy of honor, such as certain athletes, ministers, and Bible heroes. If your child was named after someone, explain who it was and why you appreciate that person. You might also tell the child the meaning of his or her name.

It is vital for boys to identify with males and for girls to identify with females. Without such identification the child might become a homosexual or lesbian, if the problem is severe, or have sexual maladjustments in marriage if the problem is less severe. It is unfortunate that we do not have more male elementary school teachers. So many boys go through life with either no father or an absent father, and few other male adults in the early elementary years. Constantly surrounded by female school teachers, Sunday school teachers, baby-sitters, and so on it is no wonder homosexuality is far more common in males than in females. We strongly recommend that churches provide male Sunday school teachers, at least for the boys and preferably for the girls as well.

A healthy father figure at this age helps girls as well as boys adjust more normally in adolescence and in married life. Of course one must be careful that the men are trustworthy—some teachers, scout leaders, and so on will induce boys and girls into sexual activity (this is more common with men, but can occur among women as well). In fact these perverted people are likely to seek out these kinds of jobs, even in churches, so be careful.

In the United States, elementary-age children often come to dislike children of the opposite sex (this isn't true in many other areas of the world). This is the age of the "cooties"—kids love to talk about how awful the opposite sex is. But don't let them fool you, they will still have a favorite or two of the other gender. Sometimes children even wish they could be the opposite sex. Kids need to see that each sex has its own distinct advantages, and parents should especially emphasize the advantages of the child's gender.

Healthy sex education can encourage personality development in a positive direction. The best place for sex education at this age is in the home. It should be done little by little, over the years, by answering questions the child asks. Be sure to answer the questions truthfully, using adult terms and talking in a matter-of-fact way without embarrassment. A child should generally know all the facts of life by ten or eleven years of age. Menstruation should be explained to elementary aged girls fairly early, because the normal range for the first period is anywhere from nine to sixteen years of age (the average is about thirteen) (Willson, Beecham, and Carringon 1966, 69). It can be terrifying if a girl has her first period without knowing what is happening—she may think she is injured or bleeding to death. Of course boys do not need to know about menstruation at this age, but you might talk to them about wet dreams and masturbation by age ten or so. Generally boys reach puberty a bit later than girls—usually about thirteen to fifteen (Ziai 1969, 38). This is why seventh-grade girls are often bigger than boys.

Discipline

We have spent considerable time in the last two chapters on this topic, and most of the comments made there continue to apply through the elementary years. The Bible repeatedly emphasizes the use of the rod and reproof (see Prov. 29:15 for example). This suggests that these are important disciplinary tools, although other forms of discipline can be included from time to time.

Spanking needs to be short and immediate. If the child becomes angry, within a few minutes he or she will be over it. If children hit their parents or show any disrespect after a spanking, they need to be spanked again. If you don't demand respect when children are young, you won't get any respect when they become teenagers. When you spank, be sure it is hard enough for the child to feel pain. Of course, bruising a child is always inappropriate and we consider slapping the child's face or hitting with a fist to be child abuse. Spanking will work for any child that is not severely mentally retarded or is not using the spanking for attention, but you must be consistent. Our experience is that within a few minutes after a spanking the child usually says, "I'm sorry, daddy. I love you."

Discipline should always follow misdeeds quickly (Eccles. 8:11). It is a serious mistake for a mother to tell her child that the father will spank the child when he gets home. This is a violation of Scripture and is also wrong psychologically. The average attention span of an elementary school child is only a few minutes, and by the time the father comes home the misdeed will be long forgotten and the punishment will have lost its effectiveness. Second, if the father does all the punishing the child may develop a distorted picture of God, since—at least at the unconscious level—experience with the father colors our picture of God. Some mothers have the father do all the discipline because they want to separate the children from the father, winning the child's undivided relationship. This is extremely unhealthy psychologically.

During the school years, parents also need to continue the earlier practice of rewarding good, productive behavior. In fact, child psychologist Erik Erikson (1963) felt this is one of the most important aspects of child-rearing at this age. The rewards do not always need to be material, however. Because children begin to think more about the reactions of their peers, you might use time with friends as a reward. However, it is important to avoid excessive shame in front of the child's friends. Discipline should generally be a private matter between the child and parent. Spanking should be discontinued at about eleven or twelve and the parent needs to use more reasoning and adult-to-adult style communication.

Reasoning with the Child

Sometimes verbal reproof is all that is necessary for elementary aged children, especially if the child is committing a particular offense for the first time. Sometimes reproof becomes even more effective if you follow it by sending the child to his or her room to think it over for five minutes. Abstract reasoning about right and wrong is usually not very helpful until the child is ten or eleven because of limitations in thinking ability. However, simple concrete reasoning can sometimes be quite effective at this age. A few kids start reasoning abstractly before age ten, but most do not.

What kind of reasoning is most effective? This tends to vary with the age of the child. Ted Ward (1979) believes that we should use the moral reasoning of the child to help us in discipline. Ward notes that Kohlberg (1985), the well-known researcher in this area, found that young children often talk about obedience and punishment when asked why they make decisions. A bit later they add more positive reasons for doing the right thing, but they are still self-centered and emphasize what they will get out of the situation. They say people should do what is right because they will receive something good and right in return ("I'll scratch your back if you'll scratch mine").

Since kids naturally begin thinking this way during early childhood, it might be best to use this kind of reasoning in discipline. For example, four- and five-year-olds will understand that they need to obey because they will be punished otherwise. But many six- and seven-year-olds will begin to understand that doing what they should can be rewarding. In addition they can begin to see that if they are nice to others, other people are more likely to be good to them. They can see the logic of Daddy being more likely to play with them if they obey Daddy and let him read the paper without interruption for a few minutes.

Kohlberg found that in the late elementary years, by age nine or ten, children begin to reason morally in a more advanced way. The approval of others becomes more and more important. As a result, if they are developing in a healthy manner, they will appreciate the smile of parents (or friends) more than some specific reward. Of course, if they never get approval from parents this level of reasoning may not develop, or they will only seek approval from their friends. Children want to be seen as "good boys and girls." Later in adolescence, Kohlberg noted that some youngsters come to appreciate respect for authority and doing one's duty. Teenagers better understand the need for law and order.

Kohlberg's research suggests that reasoning with the older school child should emphasize social approval by parents and others. Encouraging them in being a good boy or girl might help reproof be more effective at this age. Children want the approval of others, and we may use that desire to encourage obedience and respect for parental and teacher authority. They can still appreciate rewards and punishments, and these still have a place in discipline, but our reasoning with them needs to also include an appeal to social approval.

Natural Consequences

One other method of discipline might be mentioned, the use of *natural consequences* (Dreikurs and Grey 1968). Sometimes it is best for children at this age to simply discover the natural results of their misdeeds. For example, not completing homework would result in the child receiving a failing grade. Of course, if they care nothing about grades this will not work. Another example would be that if the child spills something on the floor, he or she must clean up the mess. Sometimes natural consequences are simply the *physical* results of doing something wrong, and sometimes they would be the *logical* results of wrongdoing. Even though it can be difficult, simply allowing natural consequences to follow an act is sometimes better than interrupting natural consequences and adding another kind of punishment.

Typical Problems

Divorce or Separation of Parents

Divorce is one of the most heartbreaking things in American society today, and it is nearly always the result of one or both parents being too selfish or proud to admit that their conflicts can be resolved. If both husband and wife are willing to work at it, many of their worst problems can be taken care of. The idea of having incompatible personalities and "unresolvable differences" is pure nonsense! Any two people with normal intelligence can learn to enjoy life together if they are willing to work on their conflicts. The easy way out is for a couple with marital and psychological conflicts to divorce and remarry. But then there are *two* couples with conflicts instead of one. Jesus listed adultery as one possible reason for divorce (Matt. 5:32 and 19:9) but he did not encourage divorce even under those circumstances. We should remember the Old Testament prophet Haggai who repeatedly sought the return of his wayward wife.

As noted in the last chapter, divorce is very unsettling for children. Children who have been fatherless for two years or more have many more psychological problems than children with fathers. They often see little hope in life (Kogelschatz, Adams, and Tucker 1972). Father absence due to divorce can also affect the child's identity with his or her gender (Hetherington, Camara, and Feathermore 1983). Usually the effects of divorce are worse than the effects of marital conflicts on the children. In fact, there is evidence that divorce does not stop the hostility between the spouses—52 percent continued to have angry interactions after divorce (Cline and Westman 1971). Wallerstein and Kelly (1980) found that school-age children were particularly likely to blame themselves for the divorce, and held on to fantasies of the parents getting back together even ten years after the divorce. They also found that these kids had more problems in selecting a marriage partner later on. Divorce not only hurts children, it also hurts the divorcees—they have more psychological problems than any other group of Americans (Gilder 1974).

All parents have conflicts with one another, but they always have three choices: one that is mature and two that are immature. The mature choice is to resolve the conflicts, even if outside help from a counselor or pastor is required. The two immature choices are to continue to live together unhappily or get a divorce and live apart unhappily. Of the two immature choices, getting a divorce is definitely worse.

Death in the Family

A death in the family, either of a parent, child, or other relative, is a serious problem. But unlike divorce, which is a willful separation, a death in the family—if handled properly—can be a maturing experience for everyone involved, even though it is tragic (Anderson 1973, Dennehy 1966, Easson 1972, Hancock 1973, Saunders 1973).

When Paul Meier was a senior in high school, he had his first experience teaching Sunday school. "It was a group of eight- and nine-year-old boys. After I taught the class several months, and came to know the boys fairly well, one of them developed a very serious form of cancer. I wept bitterly when I found out about it. The boy had accepted Christ as his Savior, and was a rapidly developing young Christian. His doctors were honest with his parents and the parents were honest with their son, explaining to him the best they knew how he would not have very much longer on this earth. They told him they would miss him a great deal, but Jesus would take care of him in heaven, and they would join him some day soon and spend the rest of eternity with him. Dying children need this kind of reassurance because the greatest fear of death is not knowing what will happen afterward.

"He was allowed to grieve over his eventual separation from his parents, but soon brightened up and accepted it. I visited him frequently in the hospital. After his leg was amputated, he became the favorite of many of the doctors and nurses. He witnessed to them regularly, telling them about Jesus and his love, and how he was looking forward to living with Jesus. He had an obvious impact on the lives of those doctors and nurses. He had a powerful influence on my life as well. When he died, all who knew him grieved, but as a result of his testimony his father finally accepted Christ and became a strong Christian in the church. His older brother, a teenager, also accepted Christ." Perhaps this illustrates how "in all things God works for the good of those who love him, who have been called according to his purpose" (Rom. 8:28), even in the middle of tragedy.

Children understand death differently at different ages. Until they are five years old most children believe that death is temporary. As a result they may continually ask when they will see grandpa again after he has died. Grief with young children tends to be brief and usually more the result of imitating others than anything else (Tamminen et al. 1988). School-age children, in contrast, come to realize that death is permanent in this life, and their understanding of death is much more like that of an adult (Vianello, Tamminen, and

Ratcliff 1992). Dying children often have a more mature understanding of death than do other children.

Children, like adults, usually go through several steps during their grieving (Kubler-Ross 1969). They don't always go through these steps in this sequence, and often people will go through some of the steps several times. When people first hear about the death of a loved one, they may *deny* it. They simply do not believe it has happened. Once convinced that it is true, they often become *angry*—at God, at the doctor, at the person who died, or at someone else. Kubler-Ross also noted that dying people may try to *bargain* their way out by promising things to God in exchange for a longer life. *Depression* is also common among dying people as well as those who are bereaved.

The child who does not comprehend death may become bitter at the dying or dead parent because he or she may believe the parent chose to die and leave the child. *Guilt* is often a part of the grieving process, which is anger turned toward the self. Children may blame themselves for the death of the family member, or feel that they did not treat the person right while alive, or even blame themselves for not saying goodbye before the death. Grief not only involves these steps—denial, anger, bargaining, depression, and guilt—but also a remembering of many of the times spent with the deceased family member or friend, often accompanied by tears.

It is important for the child (or adult) to express grief openly, and not hold in feelings by pretending nothing is wrong. Unexpressed grief can lead to depression and other psychological problems that can last for many years. We have seen a number of psychological problems resolved by allowing the person to grieve over the loss of a loved one who died many years earlier. How much healthier it would be for them to have grieved in the first place! Two or three weeks of open grieving helps the healthy child go through the stages described by Kubler-Ross and therefore feel better toward

God, self, the deceased loved one, and the rest of the family. Several months of sadness and less extreme grief are to be expected, but if serious grief lasts more than a year or two, professional counseling is called for. The important thing in grieving, either for children or adults, is that one be honest about it with everyone. All involved should be allowed to grieve and certainly the dying child should be allowed to grieve. Holding back the tears is not bravery, it is a serious mistake.

Childhood Depression

If a child is seriously depressed, he or she will often become very withdrawn and frequently tearful over a period of several weeks. However, sometimes children show depression by irritability, becoming hard to get along with, or acting out aggressively. When a child has a sudden change of behavior, try to get to the root of the problem and find out what is bothering the youngster. Something needs to be done about it. The child may need to see a child psychologist or psychiatrist for several sessions, and sometimes medication is required.

Grandparents in the Home

We recommend that in general it is *not* a good idea for your parents to live in the home on a permanent basis, whether you have children or not. It is hard enough to keep normal marital conflicts resolved without having someone there to hear the arguments or even enter into them. This also goes for brothers, sisters, or other boarders. If you are married, it is best for you to live by yourselves with your children, even though one may be tempted to help out other family members. This is even more important if you have children—adding relatives and outsiders is a real disservice to your kids. The children and your spouse need your undivided attention. The best thing a newly married couple can do for the sake of their marriage is make the break from both sets of parents.

When Brenda and I were first married, we became missionaries in the West Indies. We had little money for telephone calls, so we could not even talk to our parents for several months. Today we are thankful that we were so separated for those first few months; we learned to resolve our conflicts instead of running to a mother or father for help. We are convinced that our marriage is stronger today because we separated ourselves at the beginning of our marriage. The Bible clearly states that we are to *leave* the parents and be united with the spouse (Gen. 2:24, a verse repeated many times in the Bible).

Later on, when you have children, we think it's fine to live within driving range of the grandparents. Children can have a very special relationship with grandparents who are emotionally healthy. Often they will identify most strongly with the grandparent of the same sex. If they are invalids, it may be permissible to live next door to one's parents, but even then it is crucial to maintain some distance.

The grandparents, too, are better off living in their own home or apartment. Sometimes they benefit from living in a retirement facility with other older people with whom they can relate. As Christians, it is our responsibility to see that our elderly parents are taken care of when they can no longer do it themselves. In fact, this can be a real opportunity for our children to watch us take care of our parents, teaching them to do the same for us when we are too old to take care of ourselves. We must see to it that our aging parents are cared for (1 Tim. 5:8), but this does not mean they should move in with you. If there is no other option, they should live in a basement or a separate section of the house, but preferably they should at least be next door. We have seen many families have parents move in and then regret that decision. It's hard to back out once that decision is made.

Rearing Children in Other Countries

There are different points of view on this topic, but we believe it needs to be addressed seriously. If parents are called by God to go to a foreign mission field, they should go. But they need to be sure they are *called*. A need does not constitute a call; there are needs everywhere. Increasingly it is being found that the most effective way to reach people overseas is through Christians of the particular country involved. Those who believe they are called to reach people of other cultures might also consider missionary work in the United States, "across town and down the street," with those who live in the inner city or immigrants who have never heard about Christ. All of us are called to be missionaries in some capacity, if only with our friends at work (see Matt. 28:19–20).

If you believe God has called you to live overseas, either as a missionary or "tentmaker," it is doubly important to be sure of your calling if you have children. Children who grow up in foreign countries have extra problems to face in addition to the normal ones. Many of these extra problems can be minimized by anticipating them ahead of time and discussing them openly. Special problems faced by missionary children include the following (Werkman 1972).

1. Unusual child-rearing practices and customs
2. Problems with the children's caretakers
3. Unusual sexuality within the culture
4. Special fears
5. A sense of alienation

Of course there are also advantages in being reared overseas, such as children learning a second language and understanding other cultures better (Sharp 1985). MKs (missionary kids) are also more likely to be influenced by their parents' values, at least if they are kept at home.

Often those who live in other cultures seek out special boarding schools in which to place their children. This may involve sending elementary-age children hundreds of miles away from parents for months at a time. We may be wrong, but in light of scriptural commands to care for our families (both physically and emotionally) we really cannot see how it could be God's will to leave kids in a boarding school. We have friends who disagree with us, and sometimes such children grow up to be normal, but we have counseled many people whose missionary parents "farmed them out" to boarding schools. They often suffer severely as a result of this separation from their parents. I attended college with one such person who became a devout atheist because of what he saw as parental rejection (Paul Meier has seen this happen as well).

One woman in her twenties underwent counseling because of a traumatic boarding school experience. Her parents had ministered in a dangerous area and the mission board required her to attend boarding school as a precaution. When her parents said goodbye, she sobbed uncontrollably, fearful she might never see them again. An insensitive dorm parent told her, "your crying makes it harder for your parents to obey the Lord." Her parents eventually left missionary work because of the pain of leaving their kids. What a shame that good missionaries were lost because of an unwise mission board decision. And how tragic that this young woman still suffered from that decision. There is simply no justification for inflicting such emotional scars!

A part of the problem is that too many boarding schools have uncaring or abusive houseparents (Powell 1988). But, as we saw in earlier chapters, psychological problems often result from parent-child separation, especially during the elementary years (see Ratcliff 1992b, 131–33 for a summary of the specific problems with sending children to boarding schools). Children need real parents, not parent substitutes. Our children are our first calling from God, no matter what occupation God may call us into. If God called us to go to some foreign mission field, we would definitely go, but we would choose a mission board and a mission field where we would not have to send elementary-age children to a distant boarding school. There are plenty of other alternatives that allow kids to stay at home, including home schooling, national schools, correspondence courses, computerized learning, videotaped instruction, traveling teachers, and satellite instruction. I participated in "pooled instruction" when I was on the mission field; all the missionaries took turns teaching the children at our mission, all teaching the topics they understood best (we found that everything could be covered in two to three hours of tutoring a day). As mentioned earlier, you may even want to forego schooling until the child is seven or eight. The family has to be our first and utmost calling from God.

Handicapped Children

Having a handicapped child is usually a very difficult thing for parents. These parents generally face several special problems because of the child's handicap (Robinson and Robinson 1976; also see Ratcliff 1990 for a detailed summary of parents' reactions). First there are the special arrangements for training and care that must be made for the child. Second is the need for parents to adjust their expectations of the child to a more realistic level. Third, families with handicapped children often must explain to others over and over what the problems are. Sometimes they are not asked to attend church outings and other events, or the child may be made to feel unwelcome. Sometimes children may lack self-control, although this is often the result of poor discipline being used. As noted in the last chapter, handicapped children frequently become overdependent, passive, and somewhat withdrawn. Parents may even unconsciously reward the child for being weak. Finances are often a problem in families with a handicapped child, because of extra medical and transportation expenses. These families may also stop developing because they are "stuck" in the child-rearing stage for a longer than usual time. Because of these and other problems, family members may become bitter and envious that they are not like "normal" families. Sometimes this is indirectly expressed through child neglect or abuse.

Parents should not deny the reality of the child's handicap, but they should make every effort to encourage their handicapped child's independence. He or she does not need their pity. What is needed is their genuine love and trust in the ability to overcome or cope with the handicap, and the opportunity and encouragement to become responsible. Even retarded children can be helped to grow spiritually if given special training in church (Ratcliff 1985b). As noted earlier, elementary school children are very blunt and tease one another a lot about the smallest flaws, so the handicapped child is especially likely to face such assaults. Parents and teachers should do their best to help other children see how this hurts feelings, but keeping the handicapped child away from others will only make matters worse.

We can take heart in the fact that sometimes a handicap will strengthen a person beyond what would be attained without the handicap. God gave the Apostle Paul a handicap so Paul's pride would not hold him back from accomplishing great things for the Lord (2 Cor. 12:7). John Milton wrote his best poetry after going blind. Paul Meier knows a farm boy from a small southern town who made average grades in elementary school until he was afflicted with a handicap. That handicap gave him a real determination to prove himself and succeed in life. He became the valedictorian of his high school class, attained nearly straight As in college, and has become an extraordinarily dedicated Christian doctor. He probably never would have achieved what he has without that handicap. Instead of pitying your handicapped child, try to figure out how God can use the handicap as a blessing to produce greatness.

School Phobias

A school-phobic child is afraid to go to school and stay there all day. This problem can develop for several different reasons. Sometimes it is because the child cannot bear to be away from the mother that long. These children are overly dependent on their mothers, who never allow them to exercise much independence prior to entering school. They are often the youngest of several children, which adds to the temptation to spoil them and to resist their growing up and leaving (Berg, Butter, and McGuire 1972). These children become quite manipulative, since their mothers usually let them have their own way and give them very little discipline. If this is the reason for school phobia, parents should refuse to allow them to stay home under any circumstances, even if they play sick. And the mother should not go to school with them, as many of these mothers do. If the child runs away from school and comes home, give him or her a spanking and take the youngster back to school immediately. This may have to be repeated a number of times before the will is broken. Both parents need to sit down and reexamine their roles as parents, deciding how they can discipline and love the child in a healthier way so independence and respect will develop.

Sometimes, however, there can be other reasons for school phobia that require a very different approach to the problem. Sometimes the child may simply not be used to being around other children. You may remember the example of this in chapter three where the child had never been exposed to other children. Kids need to learn some basic social skills before they can cope with a room full of children.

Occasionally children become school phobic because they have learned to fear others. If your child has had several terrifying or painful experiences in group situations, and as a result cannot tolerate being in groups of children, he or she may need special therapy to overcome the fears. On the other hand, sometimes they can get over their fears by simply being around other children who do not attack or hurt them. Sometimes it helps to begin with only a few "safe" children, and then exposing them to larger and larger groups of kids. It may also help to reward them in some way for playing with others, but be careful not to reward the fear itself. Sometimes, in this situation, a parent going to school with the child a few times *is* a good idea, as long as this does not encourage overdependence.

Finally, immaturity may be the cause of school phobia. The obvious answer in this situation is to keep them out of school for awhile, until they are mature enough to cope. Home schooling may be the best alternative for such kids. Usually these children are also a bit behind in their prereading skills (see the previous section on mental development).

In sum, school phobia can have several different causes. The important thing is to locate the specific cause in your child because that will determine the best method of overcoming that fear.

Wetting and Soiling the Bed

About 12 percent of older preschoolers, 10 percent of first graders, and 7 percent of seven-year-olds still wet their beds (Freedman and Kaplan 1967, 1380–84). Bedwetting at this age is usually due to either a small bladder or psychological conflicts. About 90 percent of bedwetting after age six is considered to be a psychological rather than a physical problem. For example, the child may have pent-up anger at the parent because the child has been encouraged to be overly dependent. On the other hand, if a doctor finds that the bladder is too small, it may be necessary to have the child hold his urine for longer and longer periods of time (up to several hours) to stretch the bladder. If the bladder is normal, it would be wise to evaluate whether you are doing things for the child that he or she could do without your help. For example, by this age the child should be able to dress and cut foods without help.

Whatever you do, do not shame a child for wetting the bed. Usually it does not happen on purpose. Don't become overly concerned about it. Just calmly have the child clean up the bed and change the sheets. But be sure the *child* does it, even if you think a small bladder is the problem. Children are less likely to feel so guilty if they clean up the mess themselves. In addition, if they unconsciously did it to get the parent upset, cleaning up the mess takes all the fun out of it so probably they will quit. Medications are also available that usually stop bedwetting, but drugs should only be used as a last resort. See a child psychiatrist if you think medication is needed. The family might also benefit from insight provided by the psychiatrist as well.

Occasional soiling is common among preschoolers, but if it continues after age five or so this is considered more serious than occasional bedwetting. Soiling is more likely when the child's parents are divorced or when the father is gone almost all the time (Bemporad, et al. 1971). Overprotective, critical parents who were overly concerned about toilet training in the toddler years are also more likely to have children with this problem. Again, psychiatric medication and family counseling are recommended. Sometimes pediatricians are also equipped to work with soiling and bedwetting problems.

Paul Meier recalls treating one ten-year-old boy who had a divorced, mentally ill mother who was cold and rejected the boy. She would wrap up his stools to show the doctor. She had delusions about them being as large as horse manure and that they would plug up her sewer system. When the boy was hospitalized, he adjusted fairly well with only one "accident" when he was not allowed to have his way. When the suggestion was made that he might do better at a Christian home for boys, the mother pretended she didn't want to lose him, but was obviously happy to get him out of the house. He was accepted and loved at the new home and emotionally matured a great deal. The mother was treated with medication and given counseling so that she and her son could live together a year or two later with a healthier home life.

Thumb-Sucking and Tics

About 20 percent of first graders continue to suck their thumbs (Freedman and Kaplan 1969, 1380–84). Thumb-sucking in older children usually is considered to be a sign of anxiety and a possible sign that the child and parents may need some counseling.

Children with perfectionistic parents sometimes develop nervous tics, such as repeated eye squints, constant clearing of the throat, head jerking, and other habits. These problems indicate a need for family counseling and possibly medication for the child.

Hyperactivity

Nine out of ten children thought to be hyperactive are boys. However, a lot of children people think are hyperactive really are not—they simply have a high normal level of activity. The difficulty is that formal schooling in the United States requires children to be quiet and inactive, which is simply impossible for these active children. Boys are far more likely to have a high activity level because they have a higher androgen (a hormone) level than girls.

Paul Meier has evaluated and treated a large number of hyperactive children. "During the evaluation I ask the parents quite a few questions about the kind of discipline they provide. Sometimes one or both parents are simply unwilling to give the child a good healthy spanking when he or she gets out of hand. Sometimes the mother selfishly wants the child to like her and therefore will not spank, even though she knows that would be for the best. In effect the child has no real limits. But children cannot stand to be without rules and limits. As a result such children will constantly misbehave and run around in order to get limits set. When parents set and enforce the rules with good discipline, most children quit testing the limits because they have the security of knowing what they are expected to do. They realize their parents care.

"In contrast with these children, about 10 to 20 percent of overly active children in my practice qualify as genuinely hyperactive. They usually have some minor problems in the functioning of the nervous system. Intelligence is often normal or above normal, but they tend to be a bit clumsy in fine movements of the fingers. They may reverse their letters when they write and have other indications of being a 'late bloomer' (see the section on mental development). Their nerves are not as well developed as other children. Again, this lack of nerve development is more common in boys because girls tend to be a bit ahead of the boys in this area. These children often have learning difficulties because they simply cannot concentrate. By the time they are teenagers most of these kids will have a normal activity level, but in the meantime they are often misunderstood and labeled as having a behavior problem, being learning disabled, or even retarded. They generally develop such a poor self-concept that they have lifelong problems that are almost impossible to remove.

"Fortunately, modern medicine can help most of these genuinely hyperactive children. Over 90 percent improve dramatically when given a low dosage of Ritalin. I have seen many of them run around my office, spin around in the chair, and even climb the drapes, but within fifteen or twenty minutes after taking the medication they are sitting in a chair calmly answering questions. At home they begin to concentrate better and at school their grades go up. These kids are a joy to treat because the parents think I am a miracle worker! Of course it is just the medicine that helps the immature nerves function as if they were mature.

"Every six months or so these children go on a 'drug holiday,' where they are taken off the medication. When the nervous system becomes mature, the child will be as calm off the medication as on it. I have never seen a child become addicted to Ritalin, nor have I seen any adverse reactions to ending it all at once. There are also some other medications that can help if Ritalin does not do the trick.

"I have even seen Ritalin calm overly active children who got that way from poor discipline. For several weeks while the child is on medication, I provide training in proper discipline for the parents, then take the child off medication as the parents begin using better child-rearing methods." It is recommended that you see a good child psychiatrist if you fear this may be your child's problem.

Homosexuality

In chapter one we considered some of the things that can lead a child into homosexual behavior. Today there is a lot of controversy about what causes this problem. Some researchers believe the brains of homosexuals are different in some way, but most of this research is seriously flawed and cannot be trusted (Knight 1992). Even if there is some physical reason, it would only *influence* people, not *cause* the behavior. It would be similar to what has been found about alcoholics: there are certain biological influences that make people more likely to be alcoholics, but the individual *chooses* whether to give in to those influences or not. Likewise, if some biological factor is ever proven in homosexuality, the person still has a choice whether to act upon that desire. But so far the researchers have not proven that biological influences exist, and probably they never will.

There are a number of childhood experiences that more clearly influence children toward homosexual behavior in later life. For example, as seen in chapter one, an unhealthy mother/son attachment in which the son becomes a little husband to the mother can influence children toward homosexuality, especially when the father is weak or absent. Sometimes mothers try to convince their children that all men are degraded and worthless, which makes boys dislike their own gender.

Sometimes homosexuals report that their first sexual experiences were with boys or men. As a result, they learn to be aroused in the presence of members of the same sex. We know that voyeurs ("peeping toms") generally learn to be sexually aroused by looking in windows because as older children or adolescents they try peeping (while they masturbate) just as a lark. However, the link between the arousal and the looking produces the voyeurism—they have to peep to be aroused. Likewise, the early homosexual experience causes arousal and convinces the youngster that he is strange and different because of that arousal. He or she labels self as homosexual and the self-labeling makes it more likely that a lifestyle of homosexual behavior will develop. They come to believe the opposite sex cannot excite them. These people need to realize that they can learn normal heterosexual arousal as well, if they simply give themselves a chance.

It is also common to find that homosexuals were sexually abused in childhood. This abuse can be by either the mother or father (most commonly a stepfather or someone the family knows). If the mother commits the incest, the child becomes repulsed by the mother's actions and therefore avoids close relationships with women in general. If the father or another male sexually abuses the child, the boy may associate the arousal with males and see himself as abnormal and unusual. Sometimes painful or unpleasant experiences with the opposite sex may incline the child toward homosexuality. This sexual problem may also be related to not identifying with the same sex parent. Interestingly, cultures with very distinct roles for the different sexes, and in which every boy has a father or father-substitute, have virtually no homosexuality (Blitchington 1980, Rekers 1982, 37–50).

As can be seen, homosexuality can result from many different kinds of experiences. Sometimes it is difficult to find any specific influence. The Bible is clear in its denunciation of homosexuality as a sin (Lev. 18:22; 20:13; Rom. 1:21–32; 1 Cor. 6:9–10; 1 Tim. 1:8–10; Jude 6–7). What is most important is that the behavior is the result of *choice*, and that homosexuals can change (Walen, Hauserman, and Lavin 1977). However, it is important to distinguish homosexual temptation and sin—temptation is not in itself a sin, but dwelling on it or yielding is sinful. In spite of homosexual temptation, people can choose to be heterosexual and practice heterosexual behavior. At the very least, homosexuals can choose to abstain from acting on their sinful desires (Matt. 19:12).

When Paul Meier was in medical school, he treated a teenage male who was a Christian but was struggling with strong desires to commit homosexual acts. "I found that this young man's father, also a Christian, spent most of his free time playing with his older son, leaving the younger boy (my patient) home with his mother. When he got to elementary school, he found himself naturally wanting to play with the girls instead of with the boys. When he turned thirteen and entered puberty, he started to have crushes on boys, as did the girls with whom he played, and to imagine homosexual acts with the boys he liked. His older brother turned out normal. The boy I treated began doing things to become more masculine and to change his way of thinking, and would not allow himself to commit homosexual acts or even to dwell on them in his mind. Becoming normal sexually was a realistic possibility for him, but he will always carry around some scars from the poor parenting he received."

Spiritual Development

Michelangelo, the famous sculptor, is reported to have made the statement, "As the marble wastes, the sculpture grows." This statement not only applies to the development of sculpture, but also to the spiritual development of children. We as parents need to chip away at the rough marble we are given, attempting to sculpt our children into Christian adults. Between the sixth and eighteenth birthdays many psychological and spiritual struggles take place, but most of them are totally unnecessary. Effective love and discipline can minimize those struggles, although they certainly will not be eliminated.

Communication is an important aspect of spiritual development in the school years. Good communication, especially with the parent of the same sex, will encourage healthy self-worth, while poor communication can seriously damage it. Communication between parents is also important—when a husband criticizes his wife, he unknowingly is tearing down the self-worth and self-confidence of daughters who identify with the mother. Likewise, when a wife criticizes her husband, she is also psychologically affecting her sons who identify with the father.

The Conscience and Salvation of Children

During the elementary school years, the conscience continues to grow and the child becomes more self-controlled as he or she imitates the parents. As noted in chapter one, however, the conscience can become overly rigid or remain immature given the wrong kinds of examples or unhealthy child-rearing practices. The conscience of the six-year-old is still much like that of the parents, primarily because he or she acts to gain parental approval and to avoid punishment. By the end of the school years, however, the child increasingly follows the morality of his friends. This need not overly concern parents, however, because if you train the child properly up to that point, he will probably choose friends who will be a positive influence.

The development of the conscience, as well as mental development, makes it possible for children this age to genuinely repent of their sins and accept Jesus Christ as Lord and Savior. We have led six-year-olds to the Lord, and both of us became Christians by the age of six. There is certainly further spiritual development as children grow older, as their salvation experience takes on new meaning, and they learn many of the theological concepts involved. But all a person needs for salvation is expressed in Acts 16:31: "Believe in the Lord Jesus, and you will be saved."

The Spiritual Lifestyle and Atmosphere of the Family

The total atmosphere of your home needs to be devotional and godly. By this we do *not* mean that the family must sit in a corner praying all day. Rather, you should love, communicate, and play with your children, showing the fruits of the Spirit in your lives, and have some good Christian music playing from time to time, geared to the age of your children. Good, wholesome secular music also has a place from time to time. Every part of our lives is sacred—even going to a ball game and eating hot dogs—because we can show our children godly attitudes and values wherever we are.

Have family devotions together. This is a must. But make it quite brief for school-age children or it will become a torture to endure rather than a happy time of sharing Christ with one another. Bedtime and mealtimes are often convenient for this—be creative. Use high quality storybooks about the Bible or that show Christian values at work. Reward your children for memorizing Bible verses, but select verses that are short and understandable to the child.

Paul Meier decided to begin his own daily Bible reading when he was ten years old, and has been doing so ever since. "There was no pressure on me from my parents to read the Bible every day, since we had family devotions together regularly. But they had prepared me during the first ten years of life to such a point that when the Holy Spirit moved me to begin personal devotions, I was willing and eager to obey."

Fathers, take your sons hiking and fishing and discuss godly children in the Bible, like little Samuel. Mothers, go shopping with your daughters and discuss the shopping techniques of the godly woman in Proverbs 31. Date your children, one-to-one, occasionally. Buy something together for someone else in the household or for someone else that is in need.

Don't sit around watching television—that is a poor Christian witness to your children, teaching them that your faith makes little difference in your life. We wonder, too, if perhaps daytime television programs might lead to depression, dissatisfaction with marriage, and undermine Christian values in parents as well as children. Could talk shows and soap operas, which constantly emphasize every sin imaginable, be contributing to mental illness in housewives?

Christian Camps

Christian camps are usually a good influence on the spiritual development of our children. Both of us have worked at Christian camps. We both had marvelous experiences. The philosophy behind good camps is that you should wear the child out all day by letting him or her have some old-fashioned fun, then the child will listen to a brief, but effective gospel message in the evening. It really is effective. Hundreds are saved each summer, and many more rededicate their lives to the Lord. We prefer this type of camp to those in which the children are forced to study the Bible all day and wish they were at home playing baseball.

Your Church Home

We have spoken at length earlier about the right kind of church. There are many churches that are unhealthy for children. Be certain that you attend a good one. Paul Meier once read an article about a man who sued the local church because his son had been terrified by the preacher's assertion that any boy with his hair below the ears was definitely going to hell to burn forever. The boy went forward when the invitation was given and a lady at the front of the church hacked his hair off with scissors. The poor boy was so frightened that his nose bled most of that afternoon. When asked about the incident, the minister replied, "But I didn't start it, the Lord did." It is so easy for people, even pastors, to push their own prejudices on others, and then make it sound like it was all the

Lord's doing. The Lord called us to go into all the world and spread the gospel (Mark 16:15), not our personal preferences.

A good church and Sunday school can have an important positive effect on your children. Long ago, Hartshorne and May (1930) found that children who are enrolled in Sunday school are more likely to be honest, cooperative, persistent, and not display undesirable behavior. Several other recent studies confirm the positive influence of Christian education in healthy churches (Hyde 1990, Tamminen 1991). School children themselves believe Sunday school is important, but they are sometimes disappointed with what they find there (Cook 1989).

The View of God, Prayer, and the Bible

Recent research (Vianello, Tamminen, and Ratcliff 1992) indicates that school-age children often see God as being more like Superman than divinity. This is probably because of the child's mental limitations—he or she simply cannot imagine God as being fundamentally more than human. Until about age twelve, most children see God as bigger and better than people in general, but not basically different from humans. Sometimes kids understand that he is invisible, or perhaps like a giant or magician. Most school-age children understand that he created the world (we wish more scientists would understand that). The fact that God knows everything tends to surface at about six or seven, the omnipotent (all powerful) aspect of God usually is understood by age eight, but the fact that God is everywhere may not be understood until about eleven or twelve.

Children during the school years often believe prayer to be a means of God serving them, giving them their wishes. The idea that prayer is devotional and a way of hearing from God is simply beyond them. School-age children can understand the reality of miracles, that God can and does directly intervene in our world, but they are usually self-centered in this belief, thinking he acts because they prayed a certain way.

These ideas may be left behind by nine or ten, however, as they develop a more mature understanding of prayer.

School-age children usually have little question about the Bible being true, and some seven- and eight-year-olds even believe God wrote it and dropped it out of the sky! But by the teen years they can begin to understand that a number of people wrote the Scriptures, guided to avoid error in their writing by the Holy Spirit. Most school-age children take everything in the Bible literally, so you may want to avoid teaching them verses like "If your right eye cause you to sin, gouge it out and throw it away" (Matt. 5:29)! But the advantage of their literalness is that these kids will tend to believe whatever you tell them about God. Just make sure you don't tell them things they are likely to doubt later on, such as "grandma flies around in heaven with big, shiny wings."

As can be seen, the child's limited reasoning and understanding at this age can have some advantages. They are unlikely to be doubters, questioning what you tell them about God. But they simply cannot understand some of the abstract things in the Bible, and their prayers will tend to be immature and self-centered. What we can do is teach them things they *can* understand and be good examples of what we want them to become. For example, we can encourage them to pray for others and show them how to pray in a less selfish manner by our example. But our prayers in front of children should generally be short and understandable to the child, and we should talk with them about the spiritual and moral aspects of things in the midst of our everyday living.

6

Adolescence

Have you ever wondered what would amaze people the most if it were the ancient Romans or Greeks who were the archaeologists, digging up the remains of our culture? What is it that would seem the strangest and most unusual thing about us? We can't be sure, but one of the things that might surprise them the most would be our idea of adolescence.

You see, in all the previous societies that ever existed, adolescence simply did not exist. It may be hard to believe, but the idea of adolescence—a time between childhood and adulthood—is only about one hundred years old. It was invented in the United States and Europe in the late 1800s, and did not become firmly established until the early part of this century (Koteskey 1991). And as different parts of the world enter the modern era with its technology and social problems, they have tended to add adolescence to their societies as well. But even today there are a number of areas of the world that have no adolescence. Like most cultures that have ever existed, children simply grew up until they came to puberty, the time when the body is fairly mature and they can have children, and at that point kids turned into adults.

If you look in the Bible, you find Jesus—like his Hebrew peers—going to the temple at age twelve. The purpose of this visit was to celebrate the beginning of adulthood, a ceremony today's Jewish people call the Bar Mitzvah. In every country of the world, at least until the last one hundred years, people became adults and could marry, hold down a full-time job, and have all the other rights and responsibilities of adulthood at about eleven to thirteen years of age. In fact, Koteskey shows us from ancient historical records that people were considered fairly strange if they *didn't* do most of these things by the early to midteen years. Yes, our idea of a time period between childhood and adulthood would have seemed very strange, perhaps even wicked or crazy, to people in ancient times.

Many important changes take place during adolescence. For the first four years, between twelve and sixteen, your son or daughter becomes a young man or a young woman, with an adult body, ability to have children, and a desire to run his or her own life as much as possible. Those four years are also some of the roughest years many youngsters ever face because of all the major adjustments they make. Encouraging young people to make decisions on their own and to develop spiritually can help them make those adjustments.

Physically, adolescence begins with a major growth spurt. At about the same time, youngsters reach puberty: girls begin releasing eggs once a month and boys begin producing sperm. This does not happen at a particular birthday, but occurs at different ages in different people. Just look at the typical seventh grade classroom, when kids are just entering their teen years. You will see some who are clearly children in their size and shape, but others are very much adults physically. We've seen class portraits at this age where there would be a foot or more difference in height between classmates!

The change can occur almost overnight. Paul Meier was about average height on his thirteenth birthday. "Some of my friends who were once shorter than me started maturing before I did, and they passed me by. Then my growth hormones took off and I grew ten inches in a little over a year. I was so awkward for awhile that relatives quit inviting my family over for dinner—among other things I broke glasses, a camera, and my uncle's pool cue, mostly because I misjudged how long my arms and legs were. And I bumped my head so many times on low overheads that I'm surprised I don't have brain damage as a result!"

Mental Development

Not only do children become adults physically at the beginning of adolescence, but also mentally. Jean Piaget (1967) saw adolescence as the time when most people enter the final stage of mental development. At about eleven or twelve, children begin to reason abstractly, if they are of normal intelligence and have been educated sufficiently. Some, however, never reach this stage of reasoning ability, even in adulthood. They cannot understand the hidden meanings of proverbs, such as "People who live in glass houses shouldn't throw stones." They may think that sentence literally means what it says—if you have a glass house, throwing stones might make the glass break. They do not understand other ways of understanding that proverb, such as that people who have faults (which means all of us) shouldn't criticize others.

This new kind of understanding does not come overnight. These new mental abilities gradually begin developing in the preteen years, but at first youngsters are somewhat unrealistic in using this new form of thinking. To put it another way, they become idealistic, believing they could solve all the world's problems quickly and easily if everyone would just think the way they think (Piaget 1967, 64–67). They expect both their parents and church people to accept their values, without question, and to simply do what the teen thinks is best. The adolescent's desire for love from the opposite sex is also idealistic, as you can see in a lot of popular music.

As teenagers get older and have more experience thinking on an abstract level, they usually become more realistic in their thinking. They may have the same ideals, but they learn that things are not as simple as they once thought. In fact, they realize that there would still be problems even if everyone accepted the teen's values and ideas. They realize that most people simply will not change their actions overnight, and a perfect world of "peace, love, and harmony" will elude us until Christ returns. This newly realistic view of life may develop as early as the middle teenage years, for others it comes in the twenties, and for some it is never reached.

The new thinking abilities also have some spiritual consequences. It is very common for youngsters to make commitments to Christ at this age. Sometimes these commitments are first-time salvation experiences, and sometimes they are re-commitments. Both are important. If they become Christians as children, they realize they now have new abilities—including new thinking abilities—that need to be surrendered to Christ. Youth leaders and evangelists should encourage recommitments. They are not trying to be saved over and over, but rather they are turning things over to the Lord that they simply did not have earlier in life. We should encourage them in realizing that this is a new level of commitment; some describe it as asking Christ to be Lord in one's life. The teenager can understand that Jesus should be in complete control of every area of life, something they simply could not mentally grasp during childhood.

It is important that, even as teenagers become more realistic about things, that they not leave all their ideals behind. A small group of dedicated Christian men once had an all-night prayer meeting to pray that God would call someone out of their city to help evangelize the world and provide new leadership for God's people. These men had a vision, and so did the teenage son of one of them. This young man was allowed to go with his father to the prayer meeting, and he made some real commitments to the Lord as he listened to the prayers of his father and the other men. The city in which this prayer meeting took place was Charlotte, North Carolina, and the teenager's name was Billy Graham. For years now, Dr. Graham has gone to countries that would never allow missionaries to cross their borders, and millions of people have responded to his call to become Christians. All of this came from a young person who had a vision as a teenager. D. L. Moody once made the statement that "the world has yet to see what God can do through a man who is totally committed to him." Might your son or daughter be the Billy Graham of the next generation?

Social and Emotional Characteristics

Prior to adolescence, children want very much for their parents to love them, and they often do a fairly good job of staying in line with parental wishes. Peers become more important during early adolescence, with their influence peaking at eleven to twelve years of age (Costanzo and Shaw 1966). From that point onward, the influence of peers slowly decreases until most people are fairly self-sufficient by the late teen years. The strong emphasis upon peers is often difficult for parents, but they should remember that if they have brought up the child in a healthy manner, he or she will almost always choose peers who believe the same things as the parent and teenager. The interpersonal relationships developed during adolescence may very well be as important, or even more important, than what is learned in the school classroom. Emotional problems are often the result of not having satisfying relationships with others during adolescence (Segal 1967, 173).

While older children often go through a stage when they hate the opposite sex, except for perhaps a favorite or two, by the teen years most boys have decided that girls aren't so bad after all! In fact it's hard to think about anything else. As boys spend more time with girls at home and church, it may break up some of their old friendships—especially with boys who aren't interested in girls yet. Peer groups are rearranged, and sometimes these adolescents have mixed feelings about people of both sexes. Boys who were once friends may start to compete with one another for the attention of girls, and the gals try to outdo one another to grab the attention of a favorite fellow. Best friends of the same gender may become bitter enemies as a result.

Emotions often swing wildly from one extreme to the other during adolescence. In girls, this is often linked with the menstrual cycle, which gradually becomes more and more regular. Because of the fluctuating hormone levels, the female teenager is more likely to want to share love with others during the first two weeks of her cycle. For the next two weeks, she feels less secure and needs to be assured that others love her. Then for a few days before menses she may become irritable, moody, and hard to get along with (this is worse for some girls than others). But she should not be pampered too much, even during those few days. If she learns to endure this time in adolescence, it may well be easier for her the rest of her life.

Personality Development

Adolescents often ask themselves the question, "Who am I?" During the teen years a healthy local church can be a positive influence on adolescents as they struggle to create their own identities and guidelines to live by.

Erik Erikson (1963) saw teenagers as either developing personal identity or role confusion. In other words, either they come to understand who they are or they will be confused about personal identity for the rest of life. Developing an identity often involves questioning many of the basics of society, morality and faith. If teenagers have not been provided with moral guidelines earlier, they have little to question, and thus they can give up trying to find an identity. Some even commit suicide.

All the questioning and searching that teenagers experience is difficult for parents, but it is tough on the teenager as well. In the process they develop an idea of who they really are, in contrast to what their parents, or friends, or church say they should be. This is important because, as we shall see later, they are questioning their old foundations so they can lay new foundations. If this is successful, they will have a new and vibrant faith of their own, not a faith that is borrowed from other people.

Communication

One of the most important things parents can do is keep the lines of communication open. Forcing and pushing the youngster into what we want them to think and believe will tend to either produce rebellion or blind acceptance (which may produce later rebellion). If we want them to have a mature faith, we need to accept their questioning, and nudge them in the right direction when we can. Parents and churches need to encourage their thinking, and even accept their doubts, if we want them to become mature Christians. If they become threatened by our reactions, they may reject our faith and values when they leave home. Keep communicating, even if you can't agree with everything they say!

Sometimes parents will temporarily become more like their adolescents at this time, acting as *they* did during adolescence. This is usually quite healthy, making it more likely that parents will better understand and feel for their teenager. This helps communication. On the other hand, parents who imitate the latest teen styles and lingo may not really be better communicators—parents need to be themselves to be respected. The opposite reaction, of parents becoming more rigid in reaction to the teenager, is even more likely to end healthy communication. Stability at home is important for teenagers at this age.

Unless parents are especially careful, what used to be the family home can become a pit stop, used briefly by teenage sons and daughters for refueling their stomachs and sleeping! One thing that parents can do to avoid this is to have weekly family meetings in which all of the family make constructive criticisms and suggestions. As Amos asked, "Do two walk together unless they have agreed to do so?" (Amos 3:3).

To walk together with your teenagers you may have to make a real effort to communicate. But what kind of communication is needed? Research (McPherson, et al. 1973) finds that aggressive, antisocial adolescents generally have a father who pretends to be in authority in public, but in the family setting the mother is in charge and disregards her husband's opinion. These teenagers tend to "tune out" the parents. In contrast, passive, negativistic teenagers usually have fathers who give wordy lectures but disregard what the teenager has to say. Their mothers ignore them, but at least ask them an occasional question. These teenagers do not open up to their parents. Withdrawn, shy teenagers most commonly have a mother who ignores the teen and interrupts whenever the adolescent speaks. The father usually lets the mother dominate, paying attention to his wife but often interrupting the son or daughter. These teenagers pay close attention to both parents, even though the parents ignore them.

Another study of family communication (Odom, Seeman, and Newbrough 1971) found that the psychologically healthy families were more likely to communicate one-to-one, had parents who had clear roles in the family, and were less distant with one another. James Alexander (1973) similarly found that the parents of juvenile delinquents did not openly communicate and did not work at tasks with the teenager as a unified group. Families of normal adolescents, on the other hand, were very supportive of one another and were able to work together as a unit.

The communication between father and daughter can be a special problem at this age. When daughters are young, it's quite normal for the little girl to climb on daddy's lap. But in early adolescence that little girl has physically developed into a woman. This results in uncomfortable feelings in practically all fathers, and there are three major ways in which this can affect the father-daughter communication.

Some fathers feel very uncomfortable about the physical attractiveness of the teenage daughter and, not realizing these feelings are quite normal, consequently withdraw from their daughters almost completely. They may even take on an extra job to avoid being around her. She feels rejected by her father, whom she loves very much, and may begin feeling less worthwhile. Later in life she may even have a hard time feeling accepted by God or her husband because of this sense of rejection by her father.

Other fathers, those who are immature psychologically, continue to rock their daughters on their lap, so to speak, and are overly friendly with their daughters. Some even become quite seductive, with or without being aware of it. When girls or teenage women have been overly stimulated by their fathers this way, they may become sexually promiscuous. Sometimes they do not know why they are driven in this direction. Some of them even have sexual relations with their fathers (or stepfathers), which usually produces guilt feelings and hostility toward the father. They can become the histrionics described in chapter one, who unconsciously hate men and are out to prove that all men are good-for-nothings like their fathers. They will try to seduce anyone, especially good men such as pastors and missionaries, who are the ultimate proof of their theory that all men are worthless. Some of these women become prostitutes, some become lesbians, but most go from marriage to marriage, always finding out that their new husbands are worthless too, just like their fathers.

The third and healthiest way for a father to communicate with his teenage daughter is to continue to show genuine love and concern for her, including a healthy hug now and then, but without being seductive. He also openly displays affection for his wife, and the two of them together will show genuine affection for their daughter. These fathers realize that it is perfectly normal to be attracted to their daughters—after all, half of her genes come from him, and the other half came from the woman he chose to marry. He can enjoy her good looks without entertaining lustful thoughts. This serves as a basis for healthy father-daughter communication, and she may very well find a young man much like her father to marry, and be happy in that marriage. The same principle holds true for sons with their mothers: a healthy mother-son relationship may lead the son to marry a girl "just like the girl that married dear old dad," as the old barbershop song goes.

Adolescence, especially the later teen years, is the time when many begin thinking very seriously about what career they want to go into, and what they hope to accomplish in life. Men and women of this age are also thinking about what type of husband or wife they want to spend their lives with, and how they can develop their God-given talents. They may also become quite critical of their parents because they do not act according to the teen's idealistic goals. They also project their own goals and ideals on other adults, such as teachers and pastors, as well as their parents. The teen is critical of these adults because they are not living up to the expectations he or she hopes to attain some day. The older and more realistic the teen becomes, the more accepting he or she will tend to be of older adults.

Many other aspects of the adolescent's view of life will also mature in late adolescence. The young person becomes less introspective and more goal-oriented. But young people today are less goal-oriented than those in the past, preferring more pleasure and immediate gratification (Glasser 1973). In our experience this is especially true for non-Christian youths, and Armand Nicholi (1974)—a psychiatrist at Harvard University—finds a real difference in the healthy evangelical community. These young people generally have godly ideals and are willing to sacrifice themselves in many cases for the furtherance of the gospel. Evangelical young people are more likely to see themselves as pilgrims for a short time on earth, while the non-Christian young person is likely to have a smaller view of the world and his or her place in it.

Discipline

As a rule, no new kind of discipline is going to work wonders at this age. The habits developed throughout childhood are more likely to carry over and affect the teenager's actions than anything you might do now. Spanking is inappropriate for adolescents, although removing privileges or grounding the teenager are appropriate discipline methods at this age.

Negotiating and contracting is another approach to discipline that has considerable merit. It can help you stop nagging and encourage good communication between you and the young person.

The negotiating and contracting method begins with a two-hour family session involving only the teenager and both parents. During this time everyone evaluates the rules, chores, and punishments that will be involved. Have the teenager draw a line down the middle of a blank sheet of paper. Tell the teen to put specific rules and chores he or she thinks are appropriate on the left side of the line, and the punishments to be received for breaking each rule on the right side. Be sure the chores are specific regarding the day of the week on which they will be done. Surprisingly, many teenagers will be harder on themselves than their parents would be, probably because of their idealistic nature. Wanting more controls, teenagers often break rules so the parents will make them a little stricter.

After the list is made, parents should go over each of the rules, chores, and punishments listed and discuss them with the son or daughter. If the requirements or punishments are reasonable, leave them as they are. If they are too strict or too lenient, change the ones you must. As usual, the father should have the ultimate say. When you have completed the list, both parents should sign it, and the teenager should also sign it and date it.

This agreement is a contract between the teenager and the parents. If your son or daughter fails to keep the rule or perform the chore, you don't need to nag, just automatically give the consequence listed on the right side of the line. If a rule is broken, the teen suffers the consequence agreed upon.

Make the contract good for about two months and have weekly family meetings to discuss how things are going. Show respect for the teenager as a young adult, and listen to what he or she has to say, even if you disagree. When the two months are up, renegotiate the contract. If the teen has done a good job in following the contract, give a little more freedom in the new contract. If a poor job has been done, make the new contract a little stricter. This way, mature behavior is rewarded with greater freedom, while immature behavior produces more guidance and restriction. But do your best to keep the communications constructive and positive, and be sure to compliment your teenager for showing responsibility. This method has been used scores of times with teenagers and their parents, and families have usually reported that it eliminates much of the negative communication between the parents and teenager. It also helps keep the traditional parent-teenager power struggle from strangling relationships. At the same time it acknowledges the teenager as a person by valuing his or her opinions on the rules, chores, and punishments to be faced.

This method of discipline can even help adolescents deal with depression and rebellion. When it does not work, it is seldom the fault of the teenager, but rather that of the parents who fail to enforce the rules when the teenager tests them. Some parents come to counselors expecting them to cure their family conflicts and do not want to hear about the ways that *they* themselves can cure these conflicts.

Special Problems

A number of common problems plague many adolescents. For example, the hormonal changes that take place at this time produce problems with acne and body odor. Encouraging teenagers to improve their grooming habits usually takes care of the pimples and odor, but sometimes acne requires medications that can be obtained from any dermatologist. Most girls begin having periods during early adolescence, and as noted in the last chapter, they need to know about this by age eight or nine so it will not be traumatic for them.

Sexuality

God made sex and God made the desire for sex. The peak of the sex drive for the male is in the late teens, while females do not reach their peak until the early thirties. This is one reason why males have characteristically been more likely to have sexual relations during the teen years. However, in recent years teenage girls have become more and more likely to engage in premarital sex, probably because of peer pressure, pressure from boyfriends, and the constant sexual content of the media that feeds curiosity. God, who created sex, also provided a way to satisfy our sexual needs—through an intimate marriage relationship.

How common is premarital sex? While over half of teenagers have had sexual experience, this does not mean that they are having sex on a regular basis. About 40 percent of girls ages fifteen to nineteen are currently active sexually (Yoest

1992, 76). This represents a considerable increase from the past. The somewhat higher rate for boys has changed little over the last decade or so. The social acceptability of premarital sex in American society today makes it even harder for Christian young people to save themselves for marriage, as God has commanded. Parents should have talked with their children about the facts of life long before adolescence, and thus they should know about and determine to live up to God's sexual standards long before they enter the teen years. Don't force discussions about sex on your teenager, wait for him or her to bring up the subject. If you have had open communication on the topic in early childhood, this is more likely to happen. If the teen never brings it up, look for opportunities to get into a discussion on this important aspect of life.

Premarital sex was not a big problem in the Bible, or throughout most of history, because marriage often occurred by twelve or thirteen years of age. There is far more in the Bible about adultery because premarital sex was so rare, and if it did occur, it was simply expected that the couple immediately be married (and married for a lifetime). But our modern society has created adolescence, as we saw earlier, and tells teenagers they must not get married until their late teen years or—preferably—their midtwenties. What is a sexually charged teenager to do to release all the tension?

God has provided ways to relieve sexual tensions in single males, such as "wet dreams" during sleep at night. We're sure that God uses these dreams, which usually have sexual content and end with ejaculation, to release sexual tensions in a way that will not produce guilt feelings in the individual.

While we do not recommend masturbation, the Bible never mentions it specifically, although it does warn us to "abstain from sinful desires" (1 Pet. 2:11). Nearly all teenage males masturbate (some say "99 percent masturbate and the other 1 percent lie about it"), and a majority of females do this as well. Teenagers who talk to counselors about masturbation often express guilt about it, and their guilt is usually about their thoughts rather than the action itself. They would probably feel less guilt if they would stop and allow God to relieve their sexual tensions through wet dreams. Many teenagers are relieved to find out that this is not the unpardonable sin, and we let them know that some godly people think there is nothing wrong with it. It is important for fathers to talk privately with their sons about this topic, and for mothers to talk with their daughters about it. Keep an accepting attitude, and encourage them to seek the Lord's will about this matter. You might be surprised at how things like this can be a constant worry to teenagers and even adults.

Frequent social contacts with spiritually mature members of the opposite sex are also a healthy outlet for sexuality. We do not allow our sons or daughters to date anyone who is not a growing Christian (2 Cor. 6:14). A good rule is to limit dating to those who might be considered a potential spouse. Someday they will be on their own and make their own decisions, but until then we need to keep control of their dating life. Christian dating meets the needs of spirit and soul.

Christian teenagers should not be allowed to date until they have reviewed the Scriptures and written out a personal list of dating rules that are in agreement with Scripture. They should then determine in their hearts that they will never violate these rules for any reason, even if it means losing some dates. Teenagers frequently fail to realize that every individual they date will some day be someone's mate—perhaps even their own. What a teenager does or doesn't do during the dating years can significantly influence his or her future husband-wife relationship.

Parents frequently ask at what age we think a teenager is old enough to date. It all depends upon the adolescent's emotional and spiritual maturity. If your teenager is of average or above average maturity for his or her age, we recommend group dating at age fourteen, double dating at fifteen, and single dating at age sixteen. By group dating we mean activities like a young people's party at church where some of the teens may pair off after they arrive to sit or participate in games together. Allowing your teenagers to date ahead of this schedule will usually subject them to more temptations than they are able to handle. Research indicates that the earlier youngsters date, the more likely they will have premarital sex (Miller and Olsen 1986). In our opinion, a person should date a number of people of the opposite sex to evaluate what type of mate is most desired.

The Christian who says that sexual needs—spiritual, emotional, or physical—are dirty or sinful is saying that God made a mistake in creating those needs within us. This is clearly not the case—he gave us sexuality for our pleasure and enjoyment, for a means of bringing children into the world, and to help married couples become more closely bonded to one another.

When it comes to sexual matters, parents sometimes project their own (often unconscious) sinful thinking onto their teenagers, suspecting them of doing things of which they are innocent. Other parents see their teenagers as extensions of themselves. The healthiest approach, however, is to try to see things the way the teenager does, accepting him or her as a separate individual, and trying to understand the struggles that are being faced. In discussing sexual matters with your teenagers, be sure you are not projecting unwarranted suspicion, or assuming that they think exactly the same way you do.

Depression

Depression is a relatively common problem in adolescence. In teenagers psychological depression is frequently disguised. It is easy to see in adults, because a depressed adult will lose the appetite, sex drive, be wakeful at night, and have feelings of despair. But the teenager often manifests depression in other ways. Depressed teenagers may be relatively normal and then, over a period of a few weeks or months, become increasingly irritable, rebellious, and hostile, sometimes with occasional guilt feelings. This marks depression. On the other hand, if the teen has been a problem for years, depression is unlikely—sociopathic personality is more likely. Depressed teenagers are quite easy to treat in counseling. Often medications will bring remarkable improvement within a couple of weeks. This needs to be combined with counseling for the entire family, often focused on establishing good communication patterns.

Paul Meier once counseled a teenage boy who came from a Christian home. "He had been quite reasonable all his life, but in his early teens the lines of communication with his family broke down and he started getting into all sorts of trouble. He was even expelled from school. He resisted therapy, not wanting to take prescribed medication, and angrily walked out of my office several times when we discussed subjects he wanted to avoid. Within ten days he rededicated his life to the Lord, went to his family doctor, and handed him some money. The doctor asked him what the money was for, and the boy told him he had stolen some money out of the doctor's wallet during a visit a month earlier. This was a start on the repayment, the teen stated, and he would pay the rest back as he earned it at work." This shows that what looks like depression can be genuine guilt and conviction of sin.

If you think your son or daughter is going through adolescent depression, the first thing you should do is reestablish positive communication with a loving, accepting attitude. Compare your family rules to those of other Christian families. Frequently, parents of depressed adolescents are either too strict or too lenient. Try using the negotiating and contracting approach mentioned earlier in this chapter.

Suicide

Sometimes depression can become so severe that people consider suicide. With teenagers, suicide is linked not only with depression but often with other factors as well. Yoest (1992, 87) cites a number of statistics that indicate that teen suicide is now almost epidemic in American society, having increased 300 percent in the last forty years.

Armand Nicholi (1991, 35–36) links the huge increase in suicide among teenagers to changes in child-rearing and other aspects of the family. Single-parent families and, more specifically, the lack of a father in the home may be related to suicide. Early sexual activity and divorce of the parents are also likely to increase the risk of suicide (Orr, Beiter, and Ingersoll 1991; Harris and Wodarski 1987). Yoest (1992, 87–88) also cites studies linking adolescent suicide with drug usage, suicide education, and dysfunctional families. She recommends strong families, friendships, and spiritual faith as ways to discourage suicide among teenagers.

Another factor that may contribute to suicide is what is called the "personal fable" (Elkind 1978). Teenagers often think they are very special, and feel they are immune to bad things that happen to other people. As a result they may do things that are self-destructive, thinking that they are immortal or "it can't happen to me." For example, teens may engage in premarital sex, feeling that they could never become pregnant. The "personal fable" may account for teenagers taking grave chances with their lives, sometimes resulting in death.

Teenage Pregnancy and Abortion

Child-bearing among unmarried teenagers has been steadily increasing for many years and it is now 490 percent more likely than in the 1950s (Yoest 1992, 28). In addition 40 percent of all teen pregnancies end in abortion. As we saw earlier in this book, single parenthood is devastating for the children and makes it likely that the teenage mother will be stuck in poverty for the rest of her life (Whitehead 1993).

As many see it today, the only alternative to teenage motherhood is abortion. Abortion is granted, and sometimes even encouraged, for almost any pregnant teenager who asks for it. Abortion is seen by many as a way to avoid emotional problems, but there is plenty of evidence that girls who have abortions end up with as many and often more emotional and physical problems than those who go ahead and have the babies (Reardon 1987). Abortion is no answer to the problem, especially when there are so many childless people who have waited for years to adopt.

Anorexia

We have mentioned anorexia several times already in this book. It is a widespread problem today, especially among teenage girls. Most anorexics are above average in intelligence, are upper class socially, and are often daughters of parents in professional occupations (Crisp 1970). They frequently have fears about growing up, and especially becoming a woman (although these fears may be unconscious). Many have sexual guilt, sometimes for unfounded reasons. They frequently get along quite well until they start changing from a little girl into a young woman. Then all of a sudden they develop an unreasonable fear of being fat, and a fear of food, especially fattening food. Often the menstrual cycle ceases due to anorexia.

At first, parents often think their daughter is on a typical teenage diet, until she keeps losing and losing and losing. Some anorexics lose so much weight that they die of starvation or from physical side-effects of losing so much weight. Paul Meier saw one twenty-two-year-old anorexic who got down to thirty-eight pounds! Yet, even though they are very underweight, anorexic girls and women say they feel fat and may even look at themselves and see themselves as fat. Obviously their perception is disturbed if this occurs, and they need therapy. Many anorexics recover with counseling and medical help, but sometimes they continue to have sexual problems and difficulty becoming intimate with a man. These anorexics have convinced themselves that they should stay little girls both physically and emotionally. It is a shame that our culture overvalues thinness the way it does, which encourages this kind of psychological problem.

Running Away

Running away continues to be a common teenage problem. Psychiatrists can tell a good deal about the teenager and his or her family on the basis of runaway patterns. The spoiled, overly dependent teenager (usually a girl) will run away in order to punish her parents for not letting her have her way. But this kind of runaway will always see to it that they are caught, usually within twenty-four to forty-eight hours (Stierlin 1973, 56). They can't bear to be away from their mothers any longer than that! The mother of one of Paul Meier's histrionic teenage clients called at the office one day. "She was very worried and concerned because her daughter had run away that morning. I knew the daughter quite well, so I asked the mother what time her daughter had run away. When she told me, I glanced at my watch and told the mother not to worry about the daughter because she would probably be returning home any minute. Just as I was saying that I heard some crying over the phone, and sure enough, her dependent daughter had returned."

Teenagers who run away and stay away are usually more healthy than the ones who run away for only a day or two. On some occasions a teenager might mature more by running away than by staying in a mentally unstable home. However, we would never recommend they run away, since teenage runaways often become involved in drugs or prostitution, and family counseling is a better way of dealing with a bad home situation.

If children run away in order to make you feel guilty for supposedly mistreating them, be sure you don't reward them when they return. If this becomes a repeated problem, consider family counseling to find out why it is happening and what needs to change in the family. Often this occurs when parents are indulgent and smother the child, although conflicts with parents and difficulties with friends can also contribute to the problem (Stierlin 1973, 59). Counseling in this situation usually involves encouraging the parent and child to become more independent of one another.

Letting Go

Running away, at least with older teenagers, may be a signal that parents need to let go. Many Christian parents don't know when they should release their children. We are amazed at how many psychologically troubled people are still living with their parents at age twenty, thirty, or even older. This is especially true of alcoholics, many of whom marry several mother-types before divorcing for the last time and moving back to mother to finish their short lives.

We sometimes recommend that teenagers who have graduated from high school go several hundred miles away from home to develop their God-given talents in college. They need to learn the hard lessons of life by making the necessary mistakes and then correcting them. If parents have reared their children by God's standards up until that time, then the young people should do just fine on their own. Trust them. And if the parents have not reared their child by God's principles, most attempts to teach an eighteen-year-old something that should have been learned in childhood will be utterly futile. Let them move out to learn from life's hard knocks, and pray that God will help them mature. The greatest freedom the late adolescent can have is the freedom to fail. This is the freedom to make a mistake and to go on from there, having learned a valuable lesson by the experience. Don't kick teens when they are down. They will probably kick themselves enough when no one is looking. If they can learn to lose the fear of failure, they have learned a big lesson.

Spiritual Development

Very commonly, interest and belief in religion decline in adolescence. This has been found in several different countries and has taken place for several decades (Hyde 1990).

What is interesting about this trend is that a few religious groups have been able to keep their teenagers interested in Christianity and living out their faith. What is different about those groups? They are religions that stand apart from the culture the most: Mennonites, Pentecostals, and other sectarian groups (Sloan and Potvin 1983). Perhaps there is a message here for all Christians: the more we blend into our culture and teach young people to fit into society, the less interested they will be in our faith. Teenagers, perhaps because of their idealism, want to be part of a group that will not compromise with the world. They know that Christians should stand out in a secular society, not blend in with it. And they are right!

On the other hand, a healthy church needs to be accepting, and welcome young people regardless of their appearance. When I was a teenager I had somewhat long hair and a beard. I once visited a church where the pastor pointed his finger at me, shouting that hell was reserved for "long-haired hippies." Needless to say, I never returned to that church! We may not care for the latest fads our children and teenagers want to follow, but it is better to put up with a bit of orange hair than to lose our children forever.

We are entering an interesting period in human history today. The large majority of Americans profess a belief in God, but many feel that church attendance is optional. Those who attend are less and less likely to join a church in membership. There is also more church shopping, deciding each Sunday which church to attend based upon the immediate felt need of the day. Loyalty to a denomination, or even to a particular local church, is at a low point in American history. These and many other aspects of religious faith are considered in detail by researcher George Barna (1989, 1991).

Yet many teenagers today are interested in spiritual matters (Williams 1989) even if they don't attend every church service, and can be activated for Christian ministry. Not only can they be encouraged to participate spiritually, but also they are willing to become involved in changing society for the better (Campolo and Ratcliff 1991). Churches need to evangelize and spiritually nurture young people, but they should also encourage their natural interest in social issues. As James 2:17 states, "faith by itself, if it is not accompanied by action, is dead." We need teenagers who will put their faith to work by bringing a Christian viewpoint, as well as muscle power, to issues like world hunger and abortion.

The Occult and Demonic Influence

Unfortunately, the religious interests of teenagers sometimes go in quite the opposite direction, toward the demonic and occultic. Demonic influences in teenagers are becoming more likely today because teens open themselves up to that influence through occultic music groups, as well as the increased interest in satanism and other occultic activities. Paul Meier has studied demon possession extensively and has hundreds of pages of notes on the subject. "I have also discussed it with many missionaries who have cast out demons, usually through quiet prayer. I believe in demon possession, but thinks it is quite rare. I have had several psychotic clients and other people with severe psychological problems claim to be demon possessed, but with brief psychotherapy and medication the 'demons' rapidly disappeared. I do not believe genuine demon possession can be cured with therapy and medication; these clients were mistaken in their delusions." The Bible makes it clear that God delivering the person of the demons is the only way to deal with them.

To further illustrate how mistaken people can be about supposed demon activity, consider this experience. As a teenager, I once visited a church where nearly everyone went forward to have "a demon cast out." The screaming and jerking I observed seemed convincing at the time. A friend, who attended the church regularly, told me this happened every Sunday at the end of the morning service. The church had the idea that every problem a Christian could have was a demon, and so they decided that "deliverance" was the main reason for attending church! These people apparently fooled themselves into blaming demons for things that should have been dealt with by confession and forgiveness, rather than emotionally working themselves into hysterical behavior (see Ratcliff 1982).

Why is there such an interest in the occult by today's teens? We believe it represents a void in their lives, and they try to fill that emptiness with drugs and other wild experiences. Unfortunately, many Christian teenagers are also bored and may become more interested in emotional experiences than in spreading the gospel of Christ.

We need to give our adolescents warnings to avoid occultic activities and music. But even more important, we need to encourage them to participate in just the opposite—a healthy church with a vibrant, spiritual youth program. There are also good evangelical groups like the Navigators, Fellowship of Christian Athletes, Campus Crusade, InterVarsity, and Young Life that help fill the void by presenting the message of salvation and offering Christian activities. Spiritual experience and development is the best way to prevent interest in the occult, and good Christian music may help them avoid the demonic variety.

Spiritual Commitment

One of the best ways of keeping teenagers away from the occult is to encourage them to become deeply committed to Christ. Most teenagers are ripe for commitment. Indeed, commitment is required to achieve personal identity (Campolo and Ratcliff 1991), an important aspect of adolescence as we saw earlier in this chapter. Christianity that is dynamic and alive will interest many teenagers. Even among Christian youths, recommitments are common (given the right kind of appeal) and can help them totally dedicate their lives to Christ. They want to develop a clearer understanding of right and wrong and see the reasons and meanings in life.

Paul Meier made one of the biggest decisions of his life at sixteen years of age. "I was already a Christian from a godly home, but was still struggling with what I wanted in life. I had feelings of guilt, and feelings of confusion about what career to prepare for. I had no idea where I was going in life. I asked a man in my local church for some help. The man seemed so confident, so sure of himself. And he was genuine! That man, Dr. Bob Schindler, later became a missionary surgeon to Africa. He offered me a very clear answer that gave new direction to my life. He simply encouraged me to learn Proverbs 3:5–6, then meditate on it for awhile. I was ripe for that passage of Scripture: 'Trust in the Lord with all your heart and lean not on your own understanding; in all your ways acknowledge him, and he will make your paths straight.' I had been a Christian, but I hadn't been acknowledging God in all his ways, and I was certainly leaning on my own understanding. Alone in my bed that night, about midnight, with tears in my eyes, I recommitted my entire life to Jesus Christ—a decision I still stand on and have never regretted. When I quit struggling and finally rested in Christ, God started showing me the answers I was looking for, and gave me real peace. And so I know from experience that during the teenage years young people are ripe for spiritual commitment."

The road to recommitment is not always easy, however. Paul Tournier (1964, 5) describes adolescence as the stage of life when the young person takes off the "coat" of his parents' morality and begins "knitting" a coat of his or her own—at a time when teenagers are basically insecure about their ability to do so. Everything is open to question, creating stress and storm, until the adolescent rediscovers the treasures of faith from childhood. But this rediscovery is personalized, and he comes to "profess them as their own convictions, based upon his innermost experience," says Tournier.

Paul Meier did not have any major doubts about Christianity until he was in graduate school at Michigan State University at the age of twenty-two. "Then I began to wonder whether I believed Christianity simply because I was reared in a Christian home. That's a logical question to ask. So I studied other religions, Bible prophecy, and archaeology, and came to the conclusion that Christ really is God, and the Bible really is God's word to humankind. I renewed my vows to God, and my faith was eventually strengthened because it had become my own faith, not merely the faith of my parents. I believe I was genuinely converted when I was six years old and put my simple faith in Christ. When I was sixteen, I had a more mature way of looking at things, so my faith took on new and exciting meanings as I recommitted my life to Christ. But by the time I got to graduate school, I had exercised the scientific method of approaching things to such an extent that I needed a revamping and revitalizing of my faith. By the time I got through with medical school and into psychiatric training, my faith was so well-founded that I felt confident in discarding any psychiatric principle that in any way disagreed with Scripture.

"I am glad now that I went through those different stages of commitment to Christ at sixteen and twenty-two. It's somewhat amazing that after each struggle my doctrinal beliefs were almost exactly the same as what they were when I accepted the Lord at age six. I do not say that I was saved over and over, but rather, that my commitment deepened and took on new meaning at each point." We as parents and youth leaders in churches need to communicate a living Christianity to our teenagers, and provide proofs for why we believe the Bible. This will greatly ease this normal maturing process for our teenagers as they go through it.

Temptation

Young people have many temptations today. They are exposed to drugs and sex at an earlier age than previous generations, and are even encouraged by friends (and the media) to follow their desires. What can we do to help them resist temptation?

First, we should point out to them that we *are* able to overcome temptation (1 John 5:4). One important key is a vital exposure to the Word of God (Rom. 10:17). But our teenagers need to realize they are not fighting the battle alone. God promises to fight the battle for them if they will yield themselves totally to him. James, the brother of Christ, wrote, "Submit yourselves, then, to God. Resist the devil, and he will flee from you" (James 4:7). If the teenager is not sure if something is right or wrong, a good rule of thumb is, "When in doubt, don't!" He or she should also realize that God never tempts them to sin (James 1:13–14), which is a common misconception. God doesn't tempt us, he delivers us (2 Pet. 2:9).

Teens should memorize 1 Corinthians 10:13: "No temptation has seized you except what is common to man. And God is faithful; he will not let you be tempted beyond what you can bear. But when you are tempted, he will also provide a way out so that you can stand up under it." This verse was a tremendous help to us as teenagers, and it continues to be.

Often temptation comes because we sense a need. We should remember that, "my God will meet all your needs according to his glorious riches in Christ Jesus" (Phil. 4:19). Of course, what a young person may think is a need may simply be a want. Some areas, like sexual behavior, may seem like a need to a teenager, but are actually just a want. God gave the sex drive, not because he wants Christians to deny that drive, but because he wants us to satisfy it in his way according to his principles of love. Satan wants us to gratify that drive in a sinful manner, and the human tendency is to listen to Satan's temptation and fulfill ourselves that way. But with spiritual insight we can see how to gratify drives and needs in God's ways, which results in greater joy and satisfaction.

The Christian life is much easier if our needs and drives are fulfilled, and God wants them to be. If drives and needs are satisfied, temptation is less likely. So teach this to your children and tell them that the next time they are tempted, they should stop and think about which of their needs or drives they have not been meeting lately. Then recommend that they ask God to help them to meet that need in a way that will be pleasing to him rather than Satan. This will help them relieve a lot of guilt, and it will remind them that God loves them and is concerned about their everyday needs. Your accepting attitude will show them, at least on an unconscious level, that God is also understanding and accepting of the struggles and temptations they go through. Self-worth comes from doing what we know is right, and not doing those things that we believe are wrong. When we do things that we know are selfish and sinful, we lose self-worth. And emotional problems are sure to follow as our self-worth continues to go down.

A Christian Bar Mitzvah

Jewish people have a religious and family tradition that we think has great potential for emotional and spiritual development. We think Christians should consider using a similar custom in their homes. When a Jewish child reaches his or her thirteenth birthday, and enters the teenage years, the family has a big ceremony known as "Bar Mitzvah" for boys and "Bat Mitzvah" for girls (meaning "son" or "daughter of the commandments"). They invite all the relatives and close friends to this ceremony, and declare the child a young adult, with increased responsibilities as well as increased freedoms. The parents make a verbal contract with the child, which varies with the creativity of the parents. This is roughly equivalent to what Christ experienced when he went to the temple at age twelve (Luke 2:42).

This special ceremony, if used by Christians, could include a written contract with the child, giving some new freedoms along with some new chores and family responsibilities. You might promise not to spank anymore, since spanking is fine for children but somewhat degrading for teenagers. We prefer punishing teenagers with consequences related to the offense. You might remind the child of one's responsibilities before the Lord also, and encourage him or her to make some personal commitments to the Lord, perhaps in the area of personal devotions. But trust teens to make these decisions on their own, so they will be their commitments and not ours. Invite some relatives and close friends of the family, as well as some of your teenager's friends, whoever he or she wants to come. But don't let anyone bring gifts to this special birthday party. It has too many emotional and spiritual implications to get them all confused with materialistic gain. A Jewish friend of Paul Meier hated his Bar Mitzvah because everybody brought expensive gifts and had a wild time, almost totally ignoring him and the significance of the event.

Anyway, this is a suggestion we would like you to consider. We think it would have the additional value of reminding the parents that their child is growing up. Parents frequently forget this fact and continue treating their teenagers as though they were still little children. Teenagers can reason like adults, even though they are less mature; our communications with them should show not only our love but also our respect for them as young adults.

Family Customs

One of the things that can really help teenagers and children feel strong family ties is to include them in some family customs. We have spoken several times earlier in this book about the importance of daily family devotions of some kind. Family customs take this a step farther, and can create wonderful memories that youngsters will treasure the rest of their lives. Feel free to be creative in whatever customs you decide to include. One of the reasons Jewish families are so strong, and the Jewish identity of their children so powerful, is because of the customs they follow (Gaede 1985).

It is important that these customs be understandable to children and teens, and not be long and boring. For example, you may want to have a "blessing" in which you thank God for some specific area in each youngster's life that is improving and growing, then pray that God will continue to help them develop spiritually. Doing this every week or two can make spiritual concern very personal for each child or adolescent in your household. Lighting the dinner table candles, and reading Scripture before supper can be meaningful for children and adolescents. Singing the blessing can be a nice change of pace. Encouraging each person to think about how the Lord did something special for them during the day, or sharing a new insight gained recently, can help set a devotional tone for the supper conversation. Sharing these family customs once a week with another family can add meaning to the events. For details on these and other family customs see Mains (1987), and Gaither and Dobson (1983).

There are also seasonal customs that many families follow. Earlier in this book we talked about some of the possible customs related to Christmas. Families often have customs related to birthdays, Thanksgiving, and other holidays. Again, these regularly repeated actions help to draw the family together, and they can be passed on for generations to come.

Activities That Influence Spiritual Development

In a recent study by the Search Institute (Roehlkepartain 1993) three factors were found to influence the maturity of adolescents' faith more than anything else. The first influence is talking to parents about spiritual matters. While over 80 percent of parents wanted to talk more about faith with their children and teens, the topic was almost completely missing in daily conversations. Over half of the church teens said their fathers never spoke of religious things and one-third never talked to their mothers about it either.

The second most important influence upon the faith development of teens, according to the Search Institute study, was devotions, Bible study, or prayer in the home. Yet only one-third of church families reported having family devotions.

While they say they *want* regularly spiritual activities as a family, many families don't even find the time to eat together. Also, most parents feel inadequate to teach their teens (and children) about religious topics. They prefer to let the church do it, even though time at church is very limited and not nearly as influential in instilling faith within the family.

The third influence on teen faith development is having a project involving service to others. This is also quite rare in church families; only one-third get involved in any kind of service activity for the unfortunate.

Roehlkepartain (1993) emphasizes that children need to hear the "faith stories" of their parents. He also encourages parents to infuse spiritual topics into every area of family activity. This can seem awkward at first, but it becomes more natural with practice. He believes that churches can encourage family-based spiritual activities and discussions by holding classes where teens and parents practice talking about their faith. He also recommends church homework for children and teens that is taken home to spur religious discussions between parents and their youngsters. Parents can be encouraged to use "teachable moments" such as a death, wedding, birth, graduation, or even losing a job to reflect with teens and children about the practical difference made by one's faith.

7

When Good Parenting Is Not Enough

by Frederick L. Rowe

Most parents do their best at rearing their children. We are not perfect. We do not have perfect relationships with our mates, and we make mistakes in our relationships with our kids. But, if we love our kids and give them the basics—food, clothing, and shelter—if we teach them the difference between right and wrong, if we show them that their actions have consequences, if we try to encourage them in their strengths and set limits to keep them from going astray, we can consider ourselves good parents and our kids will do just fine. Most of the time.

But there are situations in which, for reasons we often cannot understand, we feel that we have run up against a brick wall with our kids. Despite the parents' best efforts, a daughter may be failing in school. A son may be angry and unapproachable, always getting into trouble. Two brothers may have disagreements that are disrupting and polarizing the family.

These are common yet immensely frustrating occurrences in families today. Complicating the picture is the fact that there are so many families that have split up and reorganized. Blended families, step-relationships, divorce, children dividing time between their parents, and single-parenting are just some of the situations families face. The task of deciding who is in charge of a family, and determining each person's role and responsibility, can be a problem in itself. When situations such as these arise, it may be that parents need help sorting out their problem and determining the best way to proceed.

It is easy for parents to fall into one of two extremes: pretending there is no problem, or seeing problems where none exist. In the first instance, there is often a serious problem that others in authority positions have recognized (most often school teachers or counselors) but that parents have minimized or ignored. In the second instance, one or both parents are often very conscientious and a bit overanxious. Their concerns may be due to a lack of experience, such as with the oldest child entering a new and unfamiliar developmental stage. The decision to get help for a child is often difficult and agonizing, but there are some general guidelines that can help you decide.

When Is Professional Help Needed?

Almost always, when help is sought for a child, it is the parent, or a teacher, or someone other than the child who believes that there is a problem. Parents often go through a major dilemma over deciding whether to get help or not. A mother may wonder whether her child is just "going through a stage" and will get better on her own. Perhaps this is the start of something more serious. "Have I, as the parent, done something wrong?"

Many parents feel guilty seeking help for a child's behavior problem. It is common to wonder any of the following questions: Why is my child different from everyone else's child? If I seek help, does that mean that I am a failure? Does it mean that my child is strange? Or, am I overreacting?

Wrestling through these questions is never easy, and there are no cookbook answers or simple formulas for deciding when professional help is appropriate. What follows are some general guidelines that may help you in the decision-making process.

In general, it is best to seek help if a child is having great difficulty in one of the following areas:

1. School (either in academics or behavior).
2. Peers (relationships with others of the same age).
3. Home life (behavior at home as seen by parents).

These are three arenas in which a child or adolescent must succeed in order to function effectively and develop into a healthy adult. If there is much difficulty or failure in one or more of these categories, it is best to seek help. Parents usually know when they are over their heads or beyond their coping ability. By the time they are ready to seek help, they have usually tried everything themselves. They have asked their friends for help, compared the child to their other children, and agonized over what to do. Teachers and school authorities are the best judges of children in the school setting, and if they are diligent, they will pick up on something that is more than simply a routine problem. Once a problem has been identified, they will usually inform the parents and will recommend that the child be seen by a professional if they think it is necessary.

If a child is having difficulty relating to peers, he or she is usually having difficulty in school, at home, or both. But, it is possible that a child can be compliant at home and at school, do relatively well academically, and still be isolated from peers. If this continues over a long period of time, parents need to look into why this may be happening.

In the end, it is always a judgment call of when to seek help. Every child is different, and no two situations are alike. The best general guidelines have to do with a consistent failure in one of the above areas. Parents will typically seek help if their child

1. Is extremely hyperactive and impulsive, jumping up out of his seat in school, interrupting the teacher, and speaking out of turn. He may have great difficulty focusing or concentrating on anything for more than a few seconds at a time.
2. Is depressed. She may be irritable and sad, cry frequently, have less energy than usual, and have wandering thoughts, making it difficult to concentrate. She may have difficulty sleeping at night, have little or no appetite, and have a sense of hopelessness about things getting any better.
3. Is frequently anxious or having panic attacks. For younger, school-age children, this may present itself as refusal to go to school. Such a child may have tremendous difficulty separating from his mother or participating in normal group activities. If the child is having panic attacks, he may suddenly become terrified in certain situations. He will feel short of breath, become dizzy, have sweaty palms, and experience a racing heartbeat. He may be nauseated and feel faint, or feel like he is going to die. These

episodes may cause him to avoid school or other important activities.

4. Has difficulty putting even simple thoughts together. Frequently, she does not make sense when she talks. Her behavior is odd and bizarre, and she may be hearing or seeing things that are not really there (hallucinations).
5. Has a drug or alcohol problem. Although the drug and alcohol use may not be readily apparent, there will often be certain types of behavior changes that will give clues. He may be hanging out with friends who use drugs. He may start to lose interest in school or other responsibilities. Grades may drop. He may begin to lie about even little things, and may stay out and away from home much of the time. He will become more defiant at home. Discipline does not seem to be effective, and it is difficult or impossible to find anything that will motivate him.
6. Has a sudden major drop in grades or academic failure, and the reason is unclear.
7. Is doing well in some subjects in school, but having tremendous difficulty with other subjects (e.g., a child reads well but has a tough time with math).
8. Gets into frequent fights at school and gets kicked out of classes for disruptive behavior.
9. Is alone a lot, seeming to have no friends. He either does not want to socialize or does not have the skills to do so.

Different Kinds of Counselors and Therapists

Once you decide to get help, what kind of counselor or therapist should you see for the different types of problems? There are many varieties of therapists and counselors for children's behavioral problems. The best way to describe them is by educational training.

Psychiatrists

A psychiatrist is a licensed physician (M.D. or D.O.) who has been through four years of college, four years of medical school, some type of internship (for one year) and at least three years of a psychiatric residency (a residency is on the job training, like an apprenticeship).

A child and adolescent psychiatrist is a psychiatrist who has had an additional two years of psychiatric training, called a fellowship. This is more on the job training in which he sees and works exclusively with children and adolescents.

Psychiatrists are the only types of physicians or counselors who are trained physicians. This means that they are the only type of counselor who can legally prescribe medications. Psychiatrists are trained in using medications, in diagnosing problems, and in different types of therapy. Because of their training, psychiatrists are most often used for diagnosis (figuring our what the problem is), prescribing medication when needed, and directing the team (if the child is seen by a team of mental health professionals).

Psychologists

Psychologists are called doctors, but they do not have medical training. Instead, they have a Ph.D. or a Psy.D. Usually they have had four years of college and at least four years of graduate training, specializing in psychology. Ph.D.s must write a dissertation, which is a scholarly book about research they have conducted. They have both classroom training and clinical on-the-job training. After they get their degrees, they usually have to do some type of supervised counseling before they can be licensed. Psychologists are licensed by the state in which they are practicing. Every state has different requirements, but a psychologist must usually work from one to three years in some type of on-the-job training before they can be licensed by the state.

Most psychologists who do counseling are either school psychologists or clinical psychologists. A school psychologist is an expert on learning. If your child is having difficulties in school, a school psychologist knows which type of tests to give the child so as to determine the specific areas in which the child is having trouble. When this is discovered, the psychologist will recommend approaches that will help the child learn to the best of his or her ability in the classroom.

A clinical psychologist specializes in counseling. There are many different types of counseling, and each psychology training program has a different emphasis, but counseling is an area in which the clinical psychologist is highly trained.

Psychologists are also the only type of counselors who are trained to give and evaluate formal psychological tests. They administer two different types of tests. One type can determine general intelligence (like IQ) or can help find a child's mental strengths or weaknesses. For example, Peter may be especially strong in math, but may be slow in reading. Sometimes testing can be so specific that it can help teachers do specialized teaching of children with academic difficulties. For instance, Mike has a hard time processing information that he hears. But, if the teacher writes the information on the blackboard, or Mike can see it on a sheet of paper, he will learn much faster and be able to keep up with the other students.

The other type of tests is personality tests. These tests help determine what a child is thinking and how she views the world. This type of test might be given if a psychologist wants to know how depressed or anxious a child is, or how she would be most likely to respond in a stressful situation (for example—cry, hit others, be aggressive, etc.). This type of formal testing does not give absolute answers, but it can help a psychologist understand what is going on with a child or adolescent who may be incapable or unwilling to talk about her feelings.

Masters Level Counselors

These counselors have four years of college plus one to two years of graduate training in counseling, both academic and experiential. The degree may be a Masters in Psychology, a Masters in Social Work, or a Masters in Counseling. Licensing requirements vary by state in terms of the length and content of training. Social workers may have the initials LCSW (Licensed Clinical Social Worker) after their name. In California there is a special masters level licensing called MFCC (Marriage, Family, and Child Counselor).

Masters level counselors may not prescribe medications, and they are not trained to administer formal psychological testing. Their diagnostic skills are not likely to be as strong as psychiatrists or psychologists. Their main expertise is in individual, family, and group counseling.

Qualifications and Compatibility

You are having trouble with your child and feel that something needs to be done, but who should you see? Generally, the best advice is to start with a recommendation from someone you trust who knows your child. A good place to ask for recommendations may be through your child's school, especially if it is an academic difficulty. Another source might be the pastor at your local place of worship. He may know a counselor who shares the same religious affiliation and is sensitive to spiritual issues. Sometimes your child's pediatrician or family doctor may know someone in the counseling field who is excellent.

Formal qualifications only tell a part of the story of who to choose for help with your child. The counselor should at least have a good reputation and experience working with children your child's age.

If your child has seen a counselor who recommends that the child receive counseling on a regular basis, both you and your child should be comfortable with the therapist. If not, then you should look elsewhere for therapy. Remember, as a parent, you are the one paying for the services, and you need to feel satisfied with what and whom you are getting. If ongoing counseling is the recommendation, you have a right to know what the therapist is hoping to accomplish and approximately how long he or she believes this will take. The more clearly defined the goals of counseling are, the better the likelihood that parents, child, and counselor will agree that these goals have been reached.

Different Kinds of Counseling and Therapy

Your child is playing outside. He falls and comes limping home crying. He has hurt his leg. He points to the place where it hurts the most, down near the ankle, which is starting to look swollen. You touch the area, and he screams in pain. You decide that he should see a doctor immediately, so you take him to the nearest emergency room. The doctor sees him right away and takes an X-ray. It is clearly a fracture. The doctor shows you the spot on the X-ray film, and you can see for yourself. There is no question about what will happen next. The ankle must be prevented from moving so that the fracture can heal. Your son will need to be in a cast for about six weeks. He will be fitted for crutches. No, he will not be able to play sports for several months. Yes, his friends can sign the cast. The two of you listen to the nurse give instructions about walking with the cast and about how to bathe. If he follows some simple and clear rules, and doesn't do anything foolish for the next couple of months, the fracture should completely heal. You go home relieved, and he can't wait to get on the phone to tell his friends about what happened.

Unfortunately, diagnosis and treatment of behavioral and psychiatric problems are not as straightforward as a fractured leg. But in psychiatry and professional counseling, we are dealing with the human mind and personality, which are far more complex than a broken limb. And much less is known about how the mind is supposed to work and how to fix it when it is not working correctly. As a result, there is often much disagreement among professionals concerning the nature of the problem, and there can also be disagreements about the best method of treatment. This is certainly true in adult psychiatry, and it is even more true in child and adolescent psychiatry. There is less research concerning child and adolescent problems, and getting a clear picture of the nature of the difficulty is far more difficult. Psychiatry and counseling depend upon what the patient tells the therapist about the problem. The younger the child, the more difficult it will be to obtain the necessary information.

In the mental health field, there are two broad categories of treatment: counseling and medication. Children and adolescents are usually treated in an outpatient setting, but can be treated in a hospital setting if necessary. What follows are descriptions of different types of counseling, followed by a description of different types of medication.

Individual Therapies

In individual therapy, the therapist meets with the child. Most frequently, this will occur once each week at a set time and will last from thirty minutes to one hour, most often lasting about forty-five minutes. Communication with the parents is also essential, and this can be set up in several ways. Some therapists have conversations with the therapist by phone, some have special sessions to discuss the child's progress. This may occur monthly, for example. Or, it is possible that the same therapist who sees the child individually will also see the family in family therapy.

Many different types of individual therapy exist, based on different theories about the nature of the problem and how to solve it. Some therapists use only one type of approach, while others will be trained in several different methods and will try to use the method that they believe is most appropriate to the situation. There are four major types of individual therapies for children and adolescents.

Psychodynamic Therapy

Sigmund Freud started psychoanalysis with adults in the early 1900s and developed several theories about the working of the mind. He taught about defense mechanisms (denial, projection, etc.) and theorized about the unconscious. Other theorists (including Freud's daughter, Anna) have applied and modified his theories in working with adolescents and children, but the basic goals and techniques are still the same.

The goals of this type of therapy are to help the person be able to function and enjoy life at his or her highest capacity. This gets more specific depending on the situation. Using only one type of therapy with children and adolescents is unusual. This type of therapy is probably best suited for older adolescents who are of above average intelligence and who show some insight into their behavior. The therapist tries to develop a basic trusting relationship with the child. Once this is established, the therapist tries to bring out the child's underlying feelings based on what was said in the session. According to psychodynamic theory, once the person understands (has insight into) why she behaves in a certain way, and once these feelings are brought out into the open (or conscious awareness), she will be able to change her behavior more easily.

Susan, age 17, had a problem with relationships. She was depressed and not doing well in school. Her parents sought out counseling. In therapy it quickly became apparent that Susan had a problem with older boys. She had been in a string of relationships with boys who had used her for sex and then verbally and physically abused her. Through therapy, Susan was able to disclose that her father had physically abused Susan's mother and had sexually molested Susan. Therapy, in this case, helped Susan to work through these issues. Working through the issues of abuse and molestation helped her to break the pattern of repeating the abuse in the present, through the boyfriends. Susan was able to choose healthier relationships and, as a result, her depression improved.

Play Therapy

Play therapy often relates to the same theories as psychodynamic psychotherapy. It is used with children, especially younger children. With adults or adolescents, the therapist tries to uncover the underlying (unconscious) feelings and reasons for behaving in a certain way. In play therapy, the therapist analyzes the way a child plays, the types of toys he uses, and the way he uses them as a way of bringing out the underlying feelings, so the therapist can point them out to the child. The assumption behind the theory is that, once the child has learned why he behaves the way he does, he will no longer have a need to behave in that way.

Cognitive Therapy

Cognitive therapy (CT), Rational Emotive Therapy (RET), and Cognitive Behavioral Therapy (CBT) are all variations on a similar approach. The theory behind cognitive therapy is that problem behavior and feelings come first from thinking and beliefs. So, if you change your thinking about something, it will follow that your feelings and behavior will change. The goal is simply to change problem thoughts and beliefs.

John, age 15, was referred for therapy because of being depressed and wanting to die. After some exploration, it was discovered that he would replay negative thoughts to himself over and over again in his mind. In school, he would think, "I'm a failure. I'll never be able to do well. I should just quit." And, outside of school, he would have recurring thoughts such as the following: "I'm a big, ugly nerd. No one would want to be friends with me!" In therapy, he was able to determine several specific situations that triggered these thoughts. Having accomplished this, he was taught to stop the thoughts in midsentence and replace them with: "I'm very intelligent and hard working. There is much that I can succeed at if I put my mind to it." Outside of school, he was taught to say to himself, "I'm fun to be with and have a terrific sense of humor. People have a great time around me once they get to know me." He kept notes on his progress in therapy and discovered that, as he changed his thinking to a more positive mode, his depression gradually improved.

Behavior Therapy

Behavior Therapy looks at behavior only. A behavior therapist does not try to analyze the child's thoughts or feelings, and he does not look for underlying or unconscious reasons why the child acts the way she does. Instead, the therapist typically has a session with the child and the parent (sometimes just the parent) and helps to identify the following.

1. Behaviors they would like to see more of.
2. Behaviors they would like to see less of.
3. Behaviors that are completely unacceptable and must be eliminated.

Once these have been determined, then the behaviors they would like to see more of are reinforced, the behaviors they would like to see less of are ignored, and limit-setting tactics are used for behaviors that are completely unacceptable. The older the child, the more self-directed their behavior therapy can be. The younger the child, the more the therapy techniques must be learned first by the parents. The parents, in turn, then use their newfound techniques with the child in the home environment.

In Parent Training classes, the child is not seen at all. Instead, parents learn the specifics of these behavioral techniques. They learn how to use a star chart to reward specific behaviors they would like to see more of. For example, if a parent wanted Michael to make his bed every day before school, she would reward him with a star on his star chart for every day that he made his bed before leaving the home. For every ten stars he received, Michael would get a choice of being able to watch his favorite video, or taking a special trip with Dad to get a treat at the local convenience store.

Group Therapy

Group Therapy in children and adolescents usually involves six to twelve children and one or two therapists. In an outpatient setting, groups meet once per week. Group therapy is less expensive than individual therapy. This method of treatment is especially helpful for adolescents. Developmentally, adolescents are strongly oriented toward relationships with their peers. For adolescents to discover that others in the group have the same or similar feelings can encourage them to open up and can quicken the recovery process. Groups can be generalized, but the most effective groups are often focused around a specific problem or goal that group members have in common.

Peter, a sixteen-year-old who had been repeatedly suspended from school for drug use and disruptive behavior, started attending a twelve-step group for teenage drug abusers. After stating that he did not really have any problems and was only in the group because he was "made to go," he was confronted by his peers (the other group members) as to why he had been suspended from school. After initially blaming his parents, school officials, and other students for his troubles, he admitted that his drug use was causing problems for him and that, for some reason, he had great difficulty stopping. Several sessions later, he relayed to the group that he had started staying out late and getting into trouble right after his Mom's divorce, and he was furious at his father for abandoning the family. Eventually, he was able to get tremendous support from other group members for "staying clean," and he was able to make close friends for the first time in his life.

Family Therapy

In individual therapies, the focus is on the child or adolescent who has a problem. In family therapy, the focus is on a dysfunctional family system that needs to be changed. Instead of one patient who is identified as having a problem, a family therapist analyzes the interactions between various family members and gets the family to work toward making those interactions more healthy. There are many different approaches to family therapy, but most approach the problem as a difficulty with the system instead of focusing on the individual.

Gina, a fourteen-year-old, was seen for therapy with her family because she had been increasingly defiant and out of control at home. Her parents felt that they had "tried everything" and still could not have peace in the house. After several sessions, it became apparent that Gina did something disruptive every time there was tension or conflict between her parents. The therapist pointed this out, wondering out loud if Gina was trying to save her parents' marriage by attracting all the negative attention to herself. The focus then shifted to the parents, who indeed had much stress in their relationship. It was then agreed upon by all concerned that the parents would have discussions about their differences in private. The parents came in by themselves for several sessions with the therapist, and Gina's behavior steadily improved at home.

Hospital Programs

Day Treatment

This is also called partial hospitalization. In these programs, children spend six to eight hours per day Monday through Friday in a hospital. They go home at night and on the weekends. The programs are similar to hospital or residential treatment programs, but the children do not stay overnight in the facility.

Day treatment can be used by a child who needs more intensive treatment than outpatient care can offer, but it is in a less restrictive setting than a hospital program. Day treatment can be used as a transition for someone who has been in the hospital, and who will eventually be going to outpatient treatment. Although far less expensive than a hospital or residential treatment, most insurance companies still do not have a plan that covers this form of treatment.

Inpatient Hospitalization

The types of children and adolescents hospitalized and the average length of stay in psychiatric hospitals has changed dramatically over the past several years. In most cases, a child will only be admitted to a hospital if he is an acute danger to himself (suicidal) or others (homicidal), but those who are unable to function adequately at home or school also benefit greatly from intensive hospital therapy for several weeks or longer. Once admitted to the hospital, he is often there for three weeks or less. In the hospital, he is evaluated and closely monitored by 24-hour nursing and counseling staff, and is usually seen daily by a psychiatrist. Following hospitalization, he goes back home and sees an outpatient counselor, goes into day treatment, or goes on to long-term residential treatment.

Residential Treatment

Residential treatment is a setting in which the children live over a long period of time, usually three months to one year. Programs have much variability in intensity and type of programming. This is a treatment for children who cannot be cared for at home but who do not need the intensity or restriction of being in a locked hospital.

Psychiatric Medications for Children and Adolescents

Medications are sometimes needed for children and adolescents with psychiatric problems. They are never the whole answer to the child's problem, but they may be a major part of the treatment. In attention deficit hyperactivity disorder, for example, the child's symptoms are most likely the result of a biological problem. The results from the right medication can be life-changing and dramatic. Sometimes medication will play only a small but important part in the overall treatment. And often, medication is simply not necessary. Most parents are reluctant to have their children take *any* type of psychiatric medication, and it should be used only after a thorough evaluation. But parents often do their children a disservice by insisting that their child not be on any medications for any reason whatsoever.

In the following section, medications are divided into different classes and types. This is really a reference section for those parents who have heard about different medications or have had one or more suggested by a professional. It is for general information only and should not be used to determine which medication is best to take.

Antianxiety Medications

Antianxiety medications come in three different classes or types.

Benzodiazepines

These medications are not routinely used with children and adolescents. If used at all, it is usually in low doses and for brief periods. This type of medication can be physically addictive if used in large enough doses over a long enough period of time. Sometimes these drugs cause children to be more agitated and anxious, exactly opposite the desired effect. Despite these drawbacks, they can be tremendously helpful when truly needed, such as for panic attacks.

Brand Name	Generic Name
Ativan	lorazepam
Dalmane	flurazepam
Halcion	triazolam

Klonopin	clonazepam
Librium	chlordiazepoxide
Valium	diazepam
Xanax	alprazolam

Side effects include sleepiness, difficulty concentrating, trouble with memory, and slurred speech. Blood levels of these drugs are not monitored. If the drugs are used with teenagers, they are usually in low dosages and on a temporary basis (until other ways of dealing with the problem can be found, such as behavioral therapy, a change in the environment, or other medications).

Buspar (Generic name = buspirone)

This is a relatively new antianxiety medication. It is used more with adults than with children and adolescents. It tends to be more effective for generalized anxiety than for panic attacks. It usually takes several weeks to be effective (unlike the benzodiazepines, whose effects can be felt within minutes). It is not addictive. It is clinically monitored. No blood levels are obtained with this drug. As with most other medications for children and adolescents, it should probably be discontinued briefly every year or so to see if anxiety symptoms recur.

Possible side effects include nausea, headache, nervousness, dizziness, restlessness, and insomnia.

Antihistamines

Brand Name	Generic Name
Atarax (or Vistaril)	hydrazine
Benadryl	diphenhydramine

These medications were originally developed to treat allergies. They are used in children and adolescents who have anxiety or insomnia because these medications have a calming effect and make people who take them feel sleepy. Benadryl is also used to counteract side effects of another class of medications called neuroleptics. Dosage is monitored clinically.

There are no blood levels for this medication. The drug produces its full effect with one to two hours of taking it. It is not the type of medication that needs to build up gradually in the body. These medications are not addictive. They are used only on a temporary basis (weeks to months) if needed.

Antidepressants

Antidepressants in children and adolescents may be used for depression, anxiety, attention deficit hyperactivity disorder, obsessive compulsive disorder, enuresis (bed-wetting), and sleepwalking. They come in several different classes, as follows.

Tricyclic Antidepressants

Brand Name	Generic Name
Anafranil	clomipramine
Elavil (or Endep)	amitriptyline
Norpramin (or Pertofrane)	desipramine
Pamelor (or Aventyl)	nortriptyline
Tofranil	imipramine

Common side effects are dry mouth, constipation, blurred vision, weight gain, and dizziness (which usually occurs when standing up quickly). More serious, but less common, side effects are high or low blood pressure, skin rash, heart problems, and difficulty urinating.

Because of the possibility of heart problems, an EKG is usually taken before starting the child on an antidepressant. If the EKG is normal, and there is no prior history of heart problems, then further heart problems are not likely to occur.

Most of these medications take several weeks to be effective. Blood levels can be obtained, but it is really up to the doctor whether and when he should check the blood level. The biggest danger of these drugs is that they can be lethal when taken in an overdose. Therefore, the dispensing of these medications needs to be closely monitored.

Prozac (Generic name = fluoxetine)

Prozac is a relatively new antidepressant on the market. It has become extremely popular because it is effective and has fewer, less severe, side effects than other antidepressants. It has also been used for people with obsessive compulsive disorder, Tourrette's syndrome, and children with attention deficit hyperactivity disorder. As with other new medications in psychiatry, Prozac has been tried for many disorders, but its original and primary use is as an antidepressant.

In 1991 Prozac received much negative publicity over a claim that it caused depression to worsen and caused people to have suicidal thoughts. This has not been proven and is, at worst, a rare occurrence. Close clinical monitoring is essential, as it is with other antidepressants. There are not blood levels for Prozac.

Prozac takes up to three weeks to stabilize in the body at a given dosage, which is longer than most other antidepressants. Side effects include nausea, anxiety or nervousness, weight loss, insomnia (trouble sleeping), headaches, and excessive sweating. Some people can also become restless or agitated and feel "speeded up" as if they have been taking too much caffeine.

There are no known long-term side effects of Prozac. As with other medications taken by children and adolescents, the medication should be periodically discontinued (usually once per year at the doctor's discretion) to help determine whether it is still necessary.

Atypical Antidepressants and MAO Inhibitors

Monoamine Oxidase Inhibitors (MAOIs):

Brand Name	Generic Name
Marplan	isocarboxazid
Nardil	phenelzine
Parnate	tranylcypromine

This class of antidepressants is used mainly by adults in cases of atypical depression. They are rarely used with children and adolescents. They can be just as effective as other antidepressants. The biggest problem with them is that there are certain dietary restrictions. When taking the medication, food that contains tyramine cannot be eaten. This includes things like cheese, chocolate, sausage, and other processed meats. If you can recognize how difficult it is to get an adolescent to take *any* type of medication, you can imagine the problems involved in trying to keep them from eating things like pizza and candy bars! This is why they are rarely used with this age group.

Other Atypical Antidepressants

Brand Name	Generic Name
Asendin	amoxapine
Desyrel	trazodone
Ludiomil	maprotiline

Of these agents, trazodone (Desyrel) is the only one commonly used with children and adolescents. Trazodone is most commonly used as a sleeping medication and not as an antidepressant. Sleepiness is trazodone's most common side effect, and the medication is not addictive (unlike many other sleeping medications).

Eskalith/Lithane/other brands
(Generic name = lithium)

Lithium is most commonly used by adults who have bipolar (manic-depressive) disorder. In children, it is used for bipolar disorder, but it is also used for depression, severe mood swings, or aggression. Lithium helps with several different psychiatric problems. It is also given to help *prevent* mania or depression in someone who has bipolar disorder. Therefore, in some people, it is given over many years.

Common side effects are diarrhea, nausea, vomiting, weight gain, stomachache, increased thirst, increased frequency of urination, fine hand tremor, headache, weakness, dizziness, and tiredness. Uncommon side effects are enlarged thyroid (or low thyroid functioning), acne, skin rashes, hair loss, irritability, metallic taste in mouth, and changes in blood sugar.

Lithium is a medication that can have severe side effects if too much is given. Therefore, blood levels of lithium must be closely monitored. Some side effects that can occur if too much medication is given include seizures, confusion, dizziness, slurred speech, weakness, severe trembling, vomiting, diarrhea, extreme sleepiness, irregular heartbeat, blurred vision, muscle twitches, unconsciousness.

The medication takes up to one week at a certain dose to stabilize in the body. It is not addictive. Lithium has been known to cause a partial loss of kidney function in some people who use it over a long period of time. For this reason, blood tests, including tests of kidney function, are required once or twice a year. Aside from this, there are no other long-term side effects.

Beta Blockers

Brand Name	Generic Name
Corgard	nadolol
Inderal	propranolol
Tenormin	atenolol
Visken	pindolol

These medications are used with children and adolescents to reduce aggression. They are also used for anxiety reduction, migraine headaches, and to treat restlessness that happens as a side effect from other medications (mainly neuroleptics). Side effects are tiredness, weakness, slow heartbeat, low blood pressure, and dizziness. Uncommon side effects include depression, wheezing, nausea, diarrhea, rash, muscle cramps, and insomnia (trouble sleeping).

The primary use of this type of medicine has been for blood pressure or heart problems in adults. Because of their effect on blood pressure, this must be monitored closely. An overdose of the medication could cause low blood pressure or a slowed heartbeat. Blood levels of these medications are not monitored. These medications can be used over a long period of time without harmful effects. If discontinued, however, the medication should not be stopped suddenly, but should be tapered over a period of one to two weeks.

Catapres (Generic name = clonidine)

This medication comes in two forms: pills, and a patch that is worn on the skin. This medication is primarily used as a blood pressure medicine for adults. It is now also being used to treat a variety of disorders in children and adolescents, including attention deficit hyperactivity disorder, Tourrette's disorder, and sometimes mania (bipolar disorder) or aggression. The more common side effects of this medication are sleepiness, weight gain, nausea or vomiting, dizziness, and headache. Less common side effects include depression, dry mouth, constipation, low blood pressure or pulse, nightmares, fluid retention, and swelling.

When too much of the medication is given, the biggest problems will be slow pulse and low blood pressure, since it is a blood pressure medication. Dosage is monitored according to symptoms. There are no blood tests to determine levels in the blood. This medication can be given for years with no long-term side effects.

Tegretol (Generic name = carbamezepine)

Tegretol is a medication that was originally used to treat seizures, which is still its main use. In psychiatry, however, it is most commonly used for patients with bipolar (manic depressive) disorder. In children and adolescents, it is also used to help reduce aggression and to help modify severe mood swings.

Common side effects from this medication are sleepiness, nausea, poor coordination, dizziness, and blurred vision. It can also cause temporary hair loss and can cause an increased sensitivity to the sun, requiring sun block when exposed. It can also cause a mild reduction in white blood cells, which does not cause any symptoms but is picked up in blood testing. Uncommon side effects include a decrease in some or all types of blood cells, liver or kidney damage, lung irritation, skin rash, and voice or motor tics.

Generally speaking, Tegretol has mild side effects. Most of the side effects that *do* occur are the result of either too high a blood level or too quick an increase in the dosage. Tegretol is a medication in which blood tests must be done on a regular basis, both to check the level of Tegretol in the blood and to check other bodily functions. It often takes up to a week to stabilize in the body, and it may be several weeks before it has an effect on behavior.

If properly monitored, Tegretol may be used for years without serious long-term consequences. If used for seizures or bipolar disorder, it is more likely to be needed on a long-term basis.

Neuroleptics

Neuroleptics are also called "major tranquilizers" and "antipsychotics." The different varieties are listed below.

Brand Name	**Generic Name**
Haldol	haloperidol
Loxitane	loxapine

Mellaril	thioridazine
Moban	molindone
Navane	thiothixene
Orap	pimizide
Prolixin	fluphenazine
Stelazine	trifluoperazine
Thorazine	chlorpromazine
Trilafon	perphenazine

The original and most widespread use of these medications is for adults who have disturbed thinking (psychosis). Schizophrenia is the most common illness for which these medications are used. In children and adolescents, they are used for a variety of problems, including psychosis, mania, severe depression, and Tourette's and other tic disorders. They are also used to treat severe aggression and agitation in children and adolescents who have explosive and violent episodes.

Common side effects are dry mouth, sleepiness, difficulty concentrating, dizziness, blurred vision, and weight gain. Uncommon, but more serious, side effects include enlarged breast size, stiffness in the tongue, legs, back, jaw, or other muscles, shaking of hands or fingers, inability to sit still, or restlessness. It can also cause a decrease in blood cells or damage to the liver.

The most serious *possible* side effects are neuroleptic malignant syndrome (NMS) and tardive dyskinesia (TD). NMS is very unusual but involves high fevers, confusion, extreme stiffness, and rapid changes in pulse or blood pressure. Tardive dyskinesia is a movement disorder that is involuntary. It most often involves the mouth or tongue but may include many muscles. Neuroleptics are rarely given at low doses over a short period of time. If given in high doses over many years, the likelihood increases that an individual will develop this disorder. For this reason, the use of these medications must be closely monitored by a psychiatrist.

Haldol has blood levels associated with it, but it is not entirely clear that a therapeutic blood level means the person is on the correct amount of medication. Monitoring is usually based on symptoms, not blood tests. The drug takes up to one week to stabilize in the body, but it can often take several weeks before behavioral changes occur. These medications generally should be used in low dosages and on a temporary basis.

Clozaril (Generic name = clozapine)

This medication is comparatively new. It is a neuroleptic (antipsychotic), and considered to be atypical, because the way it acts in the body is different from all the other neuroleptic drugs. It is generally used only when at least two other neuroleptics have been used over an adequate period of time in a person but have failed. It is not commonly used in children or adolescents. Psychosis is rare in children. Onset of an illness such as schizophrenia is commonly in adolescence or in the twenties. By the time psychosis has occurred, and two other drugs have been tried and failed over a period of time, the majority with a psychotic problem would already be out of childhood or adolescence.

Clozaril has several unique advantages and a few disadvantages. Unique features of the medication are as follows.

1. For people who have tried at least two other neuroleptic medications and have failed, Clozaril is effective in about 33 percent of cases. While this may seem low, it is terrific news to people with longstanding illnesses such as schizophrenia, who have not been helped by *any* medications.
2. The side effects of Clozaril are different from other neuroleptics. The good news about this is that there appears to be no evidence of tardive dyskinesia occurring in Clozaril users, which is a problem with chronic users of other neuroleptics.
3. The bad news about side effects is that this medication can cause seizures and agranulocytosis in a small percentage of users. Agranulocytosis is a condition in which the granulocytes (white blood cells) are reduced.

Since white blood cells are used to fight off infection in the body, fewer white blood cells means more infections and no way to fight them off. This could mean death in some cases.

4. Because of this disturbing possibility, everyone taking this medication must have their blood drawn weekly to check the granulocyte (white blood cell) count. If the condition is caught soon enough, it is reversible and the medication can simply be discontinued.
5. Another disadvantage of the medication is that it is currently quite expensive. Between the actual cost of the medication and the cost of monitoring it with blood draws, etc., the total cost can be as high as several thousand dollars per year, which is too expensive for many of the people who need it most. Nevertheless, for people who take it and for whom it is effective, it is a miracle drug.

Stimulants

Brand Name	**Generic Name**
Cylert	pemoline
Dexadrine	dextroamphetamine
Ritalin	methylphenidate

These medications are mainly given to children and adolescents who have attention deficit hyperactivity disorder (ADHD). This disorder has three primary behavioral components: hyperactivity, impulsiveness, and a very short attention span. Stimulants, if effective, can help with all three. Common side effects are difficulty falling asleep, poor appetite at regular mealtimes, headaches, stomachaches, irritability, and fast pulse. Uncommon side effects are muscle twitches or tics, and depression that lasts more than a few days.

There have been some misunderstandings about this medication that need to be clarified.

1. Stimulants have been shown to slow growth slightly, but this is rarely more than half an inch. Normal growth seems to resume once the medication is stopped.
2. The medication can be just as effective in adolescents as it is in children. It is even used in adults who continue to have these symptoms, and is quite effective.
3. If given to a child or adolescent who truly has ADHD, the medication will not result in a "high" and will not lead to drug addiction.
4. Children and adolescents taking stimulants do not become addicted to them. In the short acting types, the medication is effective for eight to ten hours. The medication is usually given twice daily. The first dose is in the morning, the second at noon. Sometimes a third dose is given midafternoon. This will cover the child beyond the school hours. A third dose is not routinely given because the child is more likely to have difficulty getting to sleep.

The effects of stimulants are determined by clinical symptoms and behavior. There are no blood levels for stimulants. Dosage is based on behavior. Medication is often stopped at some point during the adolescent years. The medication can be safely taken for years without significant difficulty or long-term side effects. Frequently, however, children will have "drug holidays" in which they are off the medication. This may be for as short a period of time as a weekend, or as long a period of time as a summer vacation. Because the drugs are so short acting, it takes very little time for them to build up and stabilize in the body. The advantage of this is that the medication *can* be stopped and restarted without negative effects.

8

A Final Challenge

A basic idea we have tried to present throughout this book is that parents need to work hard and do their best at child-rearing. In a sense, Christian parents are in competition with the world to produce children who become the very best in emotional and spiritual maturity. As the Apostle Paul once said, "Run in such a way as to get the prize. Everyone who competes in the games goes into strict training. They do it to get a crown that will not last; but we do it to get a crown that will last forever. Therefore I do not run like a man running aimlessly; I do not fight like a man beating the air" (1 Cor. 9:24–26).

The analogy is clear: we must do our best to get the prize. The prize Paul speaks of is spending eternity in heaven. In parenting, the "crown that will last forever," also reflects the eternal destination of our children. Taking the parallel further, we must have instruction ("training") and definite goals ("not . . . running aimlessly . . . beating the air") to complete the task of parenting. Our task is to nudge our kids in the right direction, so they will find living for Christ to be the most logical and natural way of life.

That is not to say we can ever make the decision for them. Every person ultimately must make his or her own decision for or against Christ, and be held responsible for that decision. Perhaps we sometimes give too much blame (and credit) to parents (Myers and Jeeves 1987, 36–40). No one can blame sin on his or her parents; sin is an act of the will. No one can reject Christ and then blame parents for that decision. But, on the other hand, we as parents need to give our children a positive taste for the things of God, and to encourage them in making the right decisions. What they do with the best parenting we can give them is up to them.

We have all heard the Proverb: "Train a child in the way he should go, and when he is old he will not turn from it" (Prov. 22:6).

James Dobson (1987, 184–86) has commented that this is *not* a promise, but—like most proverbs—a statement of what is most likely to result. For example, other proverbs state "diligent hands bring wealth" (10:4) and "many advisors make victory sure" (11:14). But we can think of exceptions to these and many other proverbs. Proverbs are brilliant statements of trends in human behavior, general rules that God inspired the writers to record, but not unfailing promises. Likewise, in Proverbs 22:6, God is telling us that if we do our best at parenting, we are more likely to have children who will not turn from the faith. But that is no guarantee—even God, the finest parent possible, has wayward children (Hos. 11:1–5)! We're in good company if we have struggles with child-rearing!

Mistakes in Parenting

No one has perfect parents. *We* will not be perfect parents. We have, unfortunately, made our share of mistakes. So, if you feel you have made a lot of blunders in child-rearing, well, welcome to the human race! But there is no use in dwelling on the past. Let's pick up the pieces where we are now, and develop ourselves into the very best parents our children can possibly have. Children can tolerate many parental mistakes, but the fewer we make the better for our children emotionally and spiritually. We cause psychological and spiritual handicaps in our children when we consistently refuse to cooperate with God's plan and principles. We can take heart that the general *pattern* of child-rearing is more important than occasional errors (Kagan 1979).

We encourage you to confess your past mistakes to God, remembering his promise that "If we confess our sins, he is faithful and just and will forgive us our sins and purify us from all unrighteousness" (1 John 1:9). Forgive yourself for past mistakes and move on from there with the attitude that the Apostle Paul had when he wrote, "Not that I have already obtained all this, or have already been made perfect . . . But one thing I do: *Forgetting what is behind and straining toward what is ahead, I press on toward the goal* . . ." (Phil. 3:12–14). May God reward you richly for turning from the selfish ambitions of this world and totally committing yourself to God's highest calling—being a wise, strong, loving, and godly Christian parent.

References

Adams, P. 1972. Family characteristics of obsessive children. *American Journal of Psychiatry* 128 (May): 1414–17.

Ainsworth, M., S. Bell, and J. Slayton. 1972. Individual differences in the development of some attachment behaviors. *Merrill-Palmer Quarterly* 18:123–43.

Alexander, J. 1973. Defensive and supportive communications in normal and deviant families. *Journal of Consulting Clinical Psychology* 40 (April): 223–31.

Anderson, W. 1973. A death in the family: A professional view. *British Medical Journal* 1 (Jan. 6): 31–32.

Aston, P., and G. London. 1972. Family interaction and social adjustment in a sample of normal school children. *Journal of Child Psychology and Psychiatry* 13 (June): 77–89.

Bachrach, C., M. Hown, W. Mosher, and I. Shimizu. 1985. National survey of family growth, cycle III. *Vital and Health Statistics*, ser. 2, no. 98. Hyattsville, Md.: National Center for Health Statistics.

Barna, G. 1989. *America 2000.* Glendale, Calif.: Barna Research Group.

Barna, G. 1991. *User-friendly churches.* Ventura, Calif.: Regal.

Barnes, G. 1974. Notes from his grand rounds at Duke University and residents' meeting afterward, May 2.

Baumrind, D. 1990. Effective parenting during the early adolescent transition. In *Advances in Family Research,* vol. 2, eds. P. Cowan and E. Hetherington. Hillsdale, N.J.: Erlbaum.

Belsky, J. 1988. The effect of infant day care, reconsidered. *Early Childhood Research Quarterly* 3:235–72. (A report by Belsky on this topic titled "Infant day care" is also available from the Family Research Council, Washington, D.C.)

Bemporad, J., et. al. 1971. Characteristics of encopretic patients and their families. *Journal of the American Academy of Child Psychiatry* 10 (April): 272–92.

Bennett, E. 1968. The human psyche. Lecture delivered at Arkansas State Hospital, Little Rock, Ark., November.

Bennett, E. 1971. Lecture on personality. Arkansas State Hospital, Little Rock, Ark., January 7.

Bentovim, A. 1972. Handicapped preschool children and their families. *British Medical Journal* 3 (Sept. 9): 634–73.

Berg, I., A. Butter, and R. McGuire. 1972. Birth order and family size of school-phobic adolescents. *British Journal of Psychiatry* 121 (Nov.): 509–14.

Blitchington, W. 1980. *Sex roles and the Christian family.* Wheaton, Ill.: Tyndale.

Block, J. 1969. Parents of schizophrenic, neurotic, asthmatic, and congenitally ill children. *Archives of General Psychiatry* 20:659–74.

Bolton, P. 1983. Drugs of abuse. In *Drugs and pregnancy,* ed. D. Hawkins. Edinburgh: Churchill Livingstone.

Bonine, W. 1962. *The clinical use of dreams.* New York: Basic.

Brenner, B. 1967. Patterns of alcohol use, happiness and the satisfaction of wants. *Journal of Studies on Alcoholism* 28 (Dec.): 667–75.

Brown, F., et. al. 1966. Childhood bereavement and subsequent crime. *British Journal of Psychiatry* 112 (Oct.): 1043–48.

Bruch, H. 1971. Family transactions in eating disorders. *Comprehensive Psychiatry* 12 (May): 238–48.

Bruner, J. 1986. *Actual minds, possible worlds.* Cambridge, Mass.: Harvard University Press.

Campolo, A., and D. Ratcliff 1992. Activist youth ministry. In *Handbook of youth ministry*, ed. D. Ratcliff and J. Davies. Birmingham, Ala.: Religious Education Press.

Carson, R., J. Butcher, and J. Coleman. 1988. *Abnormal psychology and modern life*, 8th ed. Glenview, Ill.: Scott, Foresman.

Cazden, C. 1972. Suggestions from studies of early language acquisition. In *Language in early childhood education*, ed. C. Cazden. Washington, D.C.: National Association for the Education of Young Children.

Chafetz, M., H. Blane, and M. Hill. 1971. Children of alcoholics. *Quarterly Journal of Studies on Alcoholism* 32 (Sept.): 687–98.

Christenson, L. 1970. *The Christian family*. Minneapolis, Minn.: Bethany Fellowship.

Clapp, R. 1984. Vanishing childhood, Part one. *Christianity Today* (May 18): 12–19.

Clavan, S., and E. Vatter. 1972. The affiliated family. *Gerontologist* 12 (Winter): 407–12.

Cleckley, H. 1941. *Mask of sanity*. St. Louis: Mosby.

Cline, D., and J. Westman. 1971. The impact of divorce on the family. *Child Psychology and Human Development* 2 (Winter): 78–83.

Coates, B., and W. Hartup. 1969. Age and verbalization in observational learning. *Developmental Psychology* 1:556–62.

Collins, G. 1971. *Man in transition*. Carol Stream, Ill.: Creation House.

Cook, S. 1989. An instrument to measure attitude toward Sunday school. *Christian Education Journal* 10:105–13.

Costanzo, P., and M. Shaw. 1966. Conformity as a function of age level. *Child Development* 37:967–75.

Crisp, A. 1970. Premorbid factors in adult disorders of weight. *Journal of Psychosomatic Research* 14 (March): 1–22.

David, H. 1981. Unwantedness: Longitudinal studies. In *Pregnancy, childbirth, and parenthood*, ed. P. Ahmed. New York: Elsevier.

Davis, D. 1991. Fathers and fetuses. *New York Times* (March 1): A27.

Dennehy, C. 1966. Childhood bereavement and psychiatric illness. *British Journal of Psychiatry* 112 (Oct.): 1049–69.

Dobson, J. 1970. *Dare to discipline.* Wheaton, Ill.: Tyndale.

Dobson, J. 1978. *The strong-willed child.* Wheaton, Ill.: Tyndale.

Dobson, J. 1987. *Parenting isn't for cowards.* Waco, Tex.: Word.

Dreikurs, R., and L. Grey. 1968. *A new approach to discipline.* New York: Hawthorne.

Easson, W. 1972. The family of the dying child. *Pediatric Clinics of North America* 19 (Nov.): 1157–65.

Elan, D. 1980. *Building better babies.* Millbrae, Calif.: Celestial Arts.

Elkind, D. 1978. *The child's reality: Three developmental views.* Hillsdale, N.J.: Erlbaum.

Elkind, D. 1981. *The hurried child.* Reading, Mass.: Addison-Wesley.

Elkind, D. 1987. *Miseducation.* New York: Knopf.

Erikson, E. 1963. *Childhood and society,* 2nd rev. ed. New York: Norton.

Evans, S., J. Reinhart, and R. Succop. 1972. Failure to thrive. *Journal of the American Academy of Child Psychology* 11 (July): 440–57.

Farnan, P. 1989. Day care diseases. *Family Policy* (May/June): 1–7.

Fish, B., et. al. 1966. The prediction of schizophrenia in infancy. In *Psychopathology of Schizophrenia,* eds. P. Hoch and J. Zubin. New York: Grune and Stratton.

Fitch, S., and D. Ratcliff. 1991. *Insights into child development.* Redding, Calif.: C.A.T. Publishing.

Ford, F., and J. Herrick. 1974. Family rules: Family life styles. *American Journal of Orthopsychiatry* 44 (Jan.): 61–69.

Formby, D. 1967. Maternal recognition of infant's cry. *Developmental Medicine and Child Neurology* 9 (June): 293–98.

Freedman, A., and H. Kaplan, eds. 1967. *Comprehensive textbook of psychiatry.* Baltimore: Williams and Wilkins.

Freedman, A., H. Kaplan, and B. Sadock. 1972. *Modern synopsis of psychiatry.* Baltimore: Williams and Wilkins.

Friedman, S. 1972. Habituation and recovery of visual response. *Journal of Experimental Child Psychology* 13:339–49.

Gaede, S. 1985. *Belonging*. Grand Rapids: Zondervan.

Gaither, G., and S. Dobson. 1983. *Let's make a memory*. Waco, Tex.: Word.

Gerber, G. 1973. Psychological distance in the family as schematized by families. *Journal of Consulting and Clinical Psychology* 40 (Feb.): 139–47.

Getz, G. 1974. *Sharpening the focus of the church*. Chicago: Moody.

Getz, G. 1975. *The measure of a church*. Glendale, Calif.: G/L Pub.

Gilder, G. 1974. In defence of monogamy. *Commentary* (Nov.): 31–36.

Glasser, W. 1969. *Schools without failure*. New York: Harper and Row.

Glasser, W. 1973. Institute for Reality Therapy. Los Angeles, Calif., August.

Golden, C. 1981. *Diagnosis and rehabilitation in clinical neuropsychology*. Springfield, Ill.: Thomas.

Goldman, R. 1964. *Religious thinking from childhood to adolescence*. New York: Seabury.

Gothard, B. 1972. Seminar: Institute in Basic Youth Conflicts. Kansas City, Mo., November.

Gothard, B. 1973. Seminar: (Advanced) Institute in Basic Youth Conflicts. Los Angeles, Calif., August.

Greenbaum, H. 1973. Marriage, family and parenthood. *American Journal of Psychiatry* 130 (Nov.): 1262–65.

Gundlach, R. 1972. Data on the relation of birth order and sex of sibling of lesbians. *Annals of the New York Academy of Science* 197 (May 25): 179–81.

Guze, S., R. Woodruff, and P. Clayton. 1972. Sex, age, and the diagnosis of hysteria. *American Journal of Psychiatry* 129 (Dec.): 745–48.

Hall, E., M. Lamb, and M. Perlmutter. 1986. *Child psychology today*, 2nd ed. New York: Random.

Hancock, S. 1973. A death in the family: A lay view. *British Medical Journal* 1 (Jan. 6): 29–30.

Harlow, H., and M. Harlow. 1965. *The affectional systems in behavior of non-human primates*, vol. 2. New York: Academic.

Harris, P., and J. Wodarski. 1987. *Social work*. Cited by N. Davidson, Life without father, *Policy review*, Washington, D.C.: The Heritage Foundation (Winter 1990): 41.

Hartshorne, H., and M. May. 1930. A summary of the work of the character education inquiry. *Religious Education* 25:607–19, 754–62.

Hawkins, D. 1975. Grand rounds on treatment of the male hysteric. Duke University Medical Center, Durham, N.C., January 16.

Hays, P. 1972. Determination of the obsessional personality. *American Journal of Psychiatry* 129 (Aug.): 217–19.

Hetherington, E., K. Camara, and D. Feathermore. 1983. Achievement and intellectual functioning of children in one-parent households. In *Achievement and achievement motives*, ed. J. Spence. San Francisco: Freeman.

Hoffman, H., et. al. 1970. Emotional self-descriptions of alcoholic patients after treatment. *Psychological Reports* 26 (June): 892.

Hoffman, H. 1970. Analysis of moods in personality disorders. *Psychological Reports* 27 (Aug.): 187–90.

Hunt, D. 1970. *Parents and children in history*. New York: Basic.

Husband, P., and P. Hinton. 1972. Families of children with repeated accidents. *Archives of diseases of children* 47 (June): 396–400.

Hyde, K. 1990. *Religion in childhood and adolescence*. Birmingham, Ala.: Religious Education Press.

Hyder, O. 1971. *The Christian's book of psychiatry*. Old Tappan, N.J.: Revell.

John, E., D. Savitz, and D. Sadler. 1991. Prenatal exposure to parents' smoking. *American Journal of Epidemiology* 133:123–32.

Kagan, J. 1979. Family experiences and the child's development. *American Psychologist* 34:886–91.

Kaplan, E., and G. Kaplan. 1971. The prelinguistic child. In *Human development and cognitive processes*, ed. J. Elliott. New York: Holt, Rinehart and Winston.

Kaye, K., and A. Wells. 1980. Mothers' jiggling and the burst-pause pattern in neonatal feeding. *Infant Behavior and Development* 3:29–46.

Kirk, S. 1972. *Educating exceptional children.* Boston: Houghton Mifflin.

Knight, R. 1992. Sexual disorientation. *Family Policy* 5 (June): 1–7.

Kogelschatz, J., P. Adams, and D. Tucker. 1972. Family styles of fatherless households. *Journal of the American Academy of Child Psychiatry* 11 (April): 365–83.

Kohlberg, L. 1985. *The psychology of moral development.* San Francisco: Harper and Row.

Koteskey, R. 1991. The social invention of adolescence. In *Handbook of youth ministry,* ed. D. Ratcliff. Birmingham, Ala.: Religious Education Press.

Kübler-Ross, E. 1969. *On death and dying.* New York: Macmillan.

Lidz, T. 1968. *The person.* New York: Basic.

Lidz, T. 1972. The nature and origins of schizophrenic disorders. *Annals of Internal Medicine* 77 (Oct.): 639–45.

Lynch, M., D. Steinberg, and C. Ounsted. 1975. Family unit in children's psychiatric hospital. *British Medical Journal* 2:127–29.

Maccoby, E., and J. Martin. 1983. Socialization in the context of the family. In *Handbook of child psychology,* 4th ed., vol. 4, ed. P. Mussen. New York: Wiley.

Mains, K. 1987. *Making Sunday special.* Waco, Tex.: Word.

Martin G., and R. Clark. 1982. Distress crying in neonates: Species and peer specificity. *Developmental Psychology* 18:3–9.

Massey, C. 1988. Preschooler moral development. In *Handbook of preschool religious education,* ed. D. Ratcliff. Birmingham, Ala.: Religious Education Press.

McCandless, B. 1967. *Children: Behavior and development.* New York: Holt, Rinehart and Winston.

McDanald, E. 1967. Emotional growth of the child. *Texas Medicine* 63 (April): 73–79.

McGrade, B. 1968. Newborn activity and emotional response at eight months. *Child Development* 39 (Dec.): 1247–52.

McNichol, R. 1970. *The treatment of delirium tremens and related states.* Springfield, Ill.: Thomas.

McPherson, S., et. al. 1973. Who listens? Who communicates? How? *Archives of General Psychiatry* 28 (March): 393–99.

Mead, M., and N. Newton. 1967. Cultural patterning of perinatal behavior. In *Childbearing: Its social and psychological factors,* eds. S. Richardson and A. Guttmacher. Baltimore: William & Wilkins.

Meier, P., F. Minirth, and D. Ratcliff. 1992. *Bruised and broken.* Grand Rapids: Baker.

Melzack, R. 1969. The role of early experience in emotional arousal. *Annals of the New York Academy of Science* 159 (July 30): 721–30.

Meredith, D., T. Timmons, and J. Dillow. 1973. Christian Family Life Seminar, Dallas, Tex.

Miller, B., and T. Olsen. 1986. Parental discipline and control attempts in relation to adolescent sexual attitudes and behavior. *Journal of Marriage and Family* 48:503–12.

Millon, T., and G. Everly. 1985. *Personality and its disorders.* New York: Wiley.

Minirth, F., et al. 1991. *Passages of marriage.* Nashville: Nelson.

Minirth, F. 1975. Hysteria—clarification of definitions and dynamics. *The Journal of the Arkansas Medical Society* 72 (Sept.): 159–62.

Moore, R. 1985. American schools: Some proven solutions. Paper for U.S. Secretary of Education for a meeting with educational leaders, June 24. Reprinted by Family Research Council, Washington, D.C. Also see his book *School can wait.*

Moore, R., and D. Moore. 1979. *School can wait.* Provo, Utah: Brigham Young University Press.

Myers, D., and M. Jeeves. 1987. *Psychology through the eyes of faith.* San Francisco: Harper and Row.

Narramore, C. 1968. *How to succeed in family living.* Glendale, Calif.: Regal.

Newton, N., and M. Newton. 1962. Mothers' reactions to their newborn babies. *Journal of the American Medical Association* 181:206–10.

Nicholi, A. 1974. A new dimension of the youth culture. *American Journal of Psychiatry* 131 (April): 396–401.

Nicholi, A. 1985. The impact of parental absence on childhood development. *The Journal of Family and Culture* 1 (Autumn): 19–28.

Nicholi, A. 1991. The impact of family dissolution on the emotional health of children and adolescents. *When families fail.* Lanham, Md.: University Press of America. (Also see his "Changes in the American family" report from the Family Research Council, n.d., Washington, D.C., and his chapter in *Family building*, 1985, ed. G. Rekers. Ventura, Calif.: Regal.)

Nichtern, S. 1973. The children of drug users. *Journal of the American Academy of Child Psychiatry* 12 (Jan.): 24–31.

Nock, S., and P. Kingston. 1988. Time with children. *Social Forces* 67 (Sept.): 59–85.

Odom, L., J. Seeman, and J. Newbrough. 1971. A study of family communication patterns. *Child Psychiatry and Human Development* 1 (Summer): 275–85.

Orr, D., M. Beiter, and G. Ingersoll. 1991. Premature sexual activity as an indicator of psychosocial risk. *Pediatrics* 87 (Feb.) 141–47.

Osborn, D., and M. Endsley. 1971. Emotional reactions of young children to T.V. violence. *Child Development* 42 (March): 321–31.

Osofsky J., and K. Connors. 1979. Mother-infant interaction: An integrative view of a complex system. In *Handbook of infant development,* ed. J. Osofsky. New York: Wiley-Interscience.

Peters, J., S. Preston-Martin, and M. Yu. 1981. Brain tumors in children and occupational exposure. *Science* 213:235–37.

Piaget, J. 1950. *The psychology of intelligence.* Boston: Routledge and Keagan.

Piaget, J. 1967. *Six psychological studies.* New York: Random.

Piaget, J. 1971. *The child's concept of time.* New York: Boston.

Powell, J. 1988. Counseling missionaries overseas. International Congress on Christian Counseling, Atlanta, Ga., November 10.

Ratcliff, D. 1980. Toward a Christian perspective of developmental disability. *Journal of Psychology and Theology* 8:328–35.

Ratcliff, D. 1982. Behaviorism and the new worship groups. *Journal of the American Scientific Affiliation* 34 (Sept.): 169–71.

Ratcliff, D. 1985a. The development of children's religious concepts. *Journal of Psychology and Christianity* 4:35–43.

Ratcliff, D. 1985b. Ministering to the retarded. *Christian Education Journal* 6:24–30.

Ratcliff, D. 1985c. The use of play in Christian education. *Christian Education Journal* 6:26–33.

Ratcliff, D. 1987. Teaching the Bible developmentally. *Christian Education Journal* 7:21–32.

Ratcliff, D. 1988a. The cognitive development of preschoolers. In *Handbook of preschool religious education,* ed. D. Ratcliff. Birmingham, Ala.: Religious Education Press.

Ratcliff, D. 1988b. Stories, enactment, and play. In *Handbook of preschool religious education,* ed. D. Ratcliff. Birmingham, Ala.: Religious Education Press.

Ratcliff, D. 1990. Counseling parents of the mentally retarded. *Journal of Psychology and Theology* 18 (4): 318–25.

Ratcliff, D. 1992a. Baby faith: Infants, toddlers and religion. *Religious Education* 87:117–26.

Ratcliff, D. 1992b. Social contexts of children's ministry. In *Handbook of children's religious education,* ed. D. Ratcliff. Birmingham, Ala.: Religious Education Press.

Reardon, D. 1987. *Aborted women: Silent no more.* Westchester, Ill.: Crossway.

Rekers, G. 1982. *Shaping your child's sexual identity.* Grand Rapids: Baker.

Rekers, G. 1986. Testimony in the U.S. House of Representatives, Select Committee on Children, Youth and Families, 99th Congress, 2nd session, February 25.

Robinson, N., and H. Robinson. 1976. *The mentally retarded child,* 2nd ed. New York: McGraw Hill.

Roehlkepartain, E. 1993. *The teaching church.* Nashville, Tenn.: Abingdon.

Rousell, C., and C. Edwards. 1971. Some developmental antecedents of psychopathology. *Journal of Personality* 39 (Sept.): 362–77.

Rutter, M. 1971. Parent-child separation. *Journal of Child Psychiatry* 12:233–60. (Also see his *Maternal deprivation reassessed*, 2nd ed. (1981/3). Harmondsworth, Middlesex, England: Penguin.)

Sagi, A., and M. Hoffman. 1976. Empathic distress in newborns. *Developmental Psychology* 12:1975–76.

Salzman, L. 1973. *The Obsessive Personality.* New York: Jason Aronson.

Saunders, C. 1973. A death in the family: A professional view. *British Medical Journal* 1 (Jan. 6): 30–31.

Schaeffer, E. 1959. A circumplex model for maternal behavior. *Journal of Abnormal and Social Psychology* 59:260–67.

Schaeffer, F., and C. Koop. 1979. *Whatever happened to the human race?* Old Tappan, N.J.: Revell.

Schickedanz, J., K. Hansen, and P. Forsyth. 1990. *Understanding children.* Mountain View, Calif.: Mayfield.

Schuckit, M. 1972. Family history and half-sibling research in alcoholism. *Annals of the New York Academy of Science* 197 (May 25): 121–25.

Segal, B., et. al. 1967. Work, play, and emotional disturbance. *Archives of General Psychiatry* 16 (Feb.): 173–79.

Sharp, L. Toward a greater understanding of the real MK. *Journal of Psychology and Christianity* 5:73–78.

Shatz, M. 1978. On the development of communicative understandings. *Cognitive Psychology* 10:271–301.

Sloane, D., and R. Potvin. 1983. Age differences in adolescent religiousness. *Review of Religious Research* 25:142–54.

Sontag, L. 1941. The significance of fetal environmental differences. *American Journal of Obstetrics and Gynecology* 42:36–39.

Spence, M., and A. DeCasper. 1982. Human fetuses prefer maternal speech. International Conference on Infant Studies, Austin, Tex., March.

Spitz, R. 1945. Hospitalism: An inquiry into the genesis of psychiatric conditions in early childhood. *The psychoanalytic study of the child,* vol. 1, pp. 53–74.

Stabenau, J. 1968. Heredity and environment in schizophrenia. *Archives of General Psychiatry* 18 (April): 458–63.

Steinburg, L., and J. Belsky. 1991. *Infancy, childhood and adolescence.* New York: McGraw-Hill.

Stierlin, H. 1973. A family perspective on adolescent runaways. *Archives of General Psychiatry* 29 (July): 56–62.

Stinett, N. 1985. Six qualities that make families strong. In *Family building,* ed. G. Rekers. Ventura, Calif.: Regal.

Strean, L., and A. Peer. 1955. Stress as an etiological factor in the development of cleft palate. *Plastic and Reconstructive Surgery* 18:1–8.

Tamminen, K. 1991. *Religious development in childhood and youth.* Helsinki: Finnish Academy of Science.

Tamminen, K., et. al. 1988. The religious concepts of preschoolers. In *Handbook of preschool religious education,* ed. D. Ratcliff. Birmingham, Ala.: Religious Education Press.

Tournier, P. 1962. *Guilt and grace.* New York: Harper and Row.

Tournier, P. 1964. *The whole person in a broken world.* New York: Harper and Row.

Vaillant, G. 1973. A 20-year follow-up of New York narcotic addicts. *Archives of General Psychiatry* 29:237–41.

Vianello, R., K. Tamminen, and D. Ratcliff. 1992. The religious concepts of children. In *Handbook of children's religious education,* ed. D. Ratcliff. Birmingham, Ala.: Religious Education Press.

Villarreal, B. 1982. *An investigation of the effects of types of imaginary play in relation to sex and temporal proximity on vocabulary and story comprehension in young Mexican-American children.* Ph.D. dissertation, The Pennsylvania State University.

Walen, S., N. Hauserman, and P. Lavin. 1977. *Clinical guide to behavior therapy.* Baltimore: Williams and Wilkins.

Wallerstein, J., and J. Kelly. 1980. *Surviving the breakup.* New York: Basic.

Wallinga, C., and P. Skeen. 1988. Physical, language, and social-emotional development. In *Handbook of preschool religious education,* ed. D. Ratcliff. Birmingham, Ala.: Religious Education Press.

Walters, C. 1965. Prediction of postnatal development. *Child Development* 36:801–06.

Ward, T. 1979. *Values begin at home.* Wheaton, Ill.: Victor.

Werkman, S. 1972. Hazards of rearing children in foreign countries. *American Journal of Psychiatry* 120 (Feb.): 992–97.

Whitehead, B. 1993. Dan Quayle was right. *The Atlantic Monthly* 271 (April): 47–84.

Williams, D. 1989. Religion in adolescence. *Source* 5 (Dec.): 1–3.

Willson, J., C. Beecham, and E. Carrington. 1966. *Obstetrics and gynecology.* St. Louis: Mosby.

Wold, P. 1973. Family structure in three cases of anorexia nervosa. *American Journal of Psychiatry* 130 (Dec.): 1394–97.

Yoest, C. (ed.). 1992. *Free to be family.* Washington, D.C.: Family Research Council.

Ziai, M. (ed.). 1969. *Pediatrics.* Boston: Little, Brown.

Zigler, E., and M. Stevenson. 1993. *Children in a changing world,* 2nd ed. Pacific Grove, Calif.: Brooks/Cole.

Index